GEORGE MICHAEL
freedom

by mick middles

First published in Great Britain in 1997 by Chameleon Books

an imprint of André Deutsch Ltd

106 Great Russell Street

London WC1B 3LJ

André Deutsch Ltd is a subsidiary of VCI plc

Printed and bound in Italy by Officine Grafiche DeAgostini.

A catalogue record for this book is available from the British Library

ISBN 0 233 99176 X

GEORGE MICHAEL freedom

contents

1 pranks and deeds at bushey meads

It was the warm, enveloping comfort of north London suburbia that provided the backdrop for the formative years of Georgios Kyriacos Panayiotou, latterly known as George Michael. Undoubtedly this story would be more neatly balanced, more poignant perhaps, had he started life in an airy stone dwelling in rural Greece, or even in a darkened East-End terraced street, but it was not so. The comforts that would surround him and his two older sisters, Yioda and Melanie, had been provided by the admirable single-minded determination of his father, Kyriacos Panayiotou – or 'Jack', as he swiftly became known – after he arrived in England, bright-eyed, optimistic and furiously ambitious, in the early 1950s. He married a working-class English girl, Lesley, when he had just one foot placed squarely on the bottom rung of the career ladder, working hard, elastic shifts as a waiter in a Greek restaurant.

Although nothing comes easy in catering, progress is, or certainly was, always in view, especially for those blessed with a ferocious work ethic. And by the time Britain entered the 1960s, Jack was enjoying a hard but lucrative life as a respected restaurateur. Steadily, the Panayiotou family floated ever upwards, out of the grip of Finchley – to Burnt Oak, Edgware, and finally, to leafy Radlett.

As such, George Michael's early life, considered of little interest by the press, was staggered by a series of jolts which, though each rendered the family increasingly comfortable, must have seemed traumatic at the time, as old

George Michael today and ...

Michael

friends would swiftly fade away, to be instantly replaced by new, potentially threatening faces. Tales of the young George are, therefore, scarce and rather dull. One might see huge significance, however, in the time when his mother, on discovering his intense fondness for pop music at the age of seven, purchased a tape recorder for him, effectively fuelling an early lust for pop stardom.

Most parents, it might be noted, would dismiss this desire, which continued to flourish into his teens, as the mere musings of a silly, childish 'pie in the sky' fantasy, but Lesley Panayiotou was apparently unswerving in her solid – and many would say naive – determination to help him have a stab at this distant goal. It was Lesley who would later push the boy towards extra, all-round painful sessions on the violin.

Although Jack continued to toil, and subsequently spent long hours away from the family abode, he was, by all accounts, pleased to see Lesley encouraging this unlikely musical bent. This was exactly the kind of opportunity he wished to see heaped upon his children. It was the reason he had worked so hard, for so many years. If this sounds most unlike the rock'n'roll norm – the petulant teenager battling against the ill-informed oppression of well-meaning parents – then, well, that's how it was. His own childhood had lacked such a romantic frisson.

In September 1975, the 12-year-old Georgios started to attend Bushey Meads School – a curious place, and something of a paradox, as it encouraged healthy lines of communication between teachers, pupils and parents while doggedly sticking, at least until 1987, to the unfashionable use of the cane. Not that this was

ever sampled by Georgios Panayiotou, a bright, generally attentive child who slipped neatly into the top stream, swiftly making allegiances with both teachers and, more tentatively, his new-found classmates. Again, one struggles to locate any degree of suitable rebellion here. No doubt it existed for, although he was generally an extremely personable child, he was physically awkward. Tall and podgy, the Georgios Panayiotou package came complete with thick-rimmed, black spectacles, quite the ultimate in mid-1970s teen anti-cool, unwittingly pre-dating the 'geek appeal' of Elvis Costello – not to mention Jarvis Cocker – by a couple of decades. In later years, Georgios would spend large amounts of time wondering about fate, remembering the day he aimlessly and, as it turned out, famously strode across the Bushey Meads playground to watch a particularly raucous game of King of the Wall taking place amid a riotous gathering of excitable pupils. The next five minutes of his life are set down in rock mythology, rather like a latterday meeting of Robin Hood and Little John, for at the centre of the 'scrum' was Andrew Ridgeley.

Dark-skinned, blessed with obscene good looks, bright, athletic, and simply overflowing with confidence, Ridgeley emitted the kind of aura that is reserved for the effortlessly cool. Already a magnet for the giggling Bushey Meads girls, Ridgeley wasted few opportunities to show off in front of them, and King of the Wall was his lunchtime show. There were few rules. One had to designate a section of wall, proclaim it utterly desirable and defend it against all-comers. Seeing Georgios lumbering past was too much for Ridgeley, who immediately began hurling jibes at him, goading him, tempting him into the game.

... in a previous incarnation as Georgios Kyriacos Panayiotou

'I'm ugly, nobody ever fancies me'

a young george michael

To most people's surprise, Georgios finally accepted the challenge and using his greater weight, shunted the stunned Ridgeley down onto the playground grit, where he sat, humiliated, dazed and apparently full of admiration. The expected rematch didn't occur. Instead, Ridgeley spent the next few days edging closer to his usurper, as if wholly fascinated by this boy who seemed to have an inner strength. Legend has since decreed that this was where the heart of the friendship was forged and, in later life, both George Michael and Andrew Ridgeley would recall the incident with a genuine degree of fondness.

Like Georgios, Andrew's character was formed in the conventional comforts of suburbia. His celebrated dark skin and film-star looks were inherited from his father, Albert Mario Ridgeley, who had crossed the divide from his Arabic origins by marrying an English schoolteacher, Jennifer. With his brother Paul, Andrew enjoyed a middle-class childhood, surging rather effortlessly through school, although his ardent precocity caused him to fall into far too many 'school scraps'. He was highly popular and, as with all popular pupils, he would incite small but vicious pockets of enemies. Envy would never be far away from Andrew Ridgeley. It was a problem that Georgios, alas, had never encountered.

As such, they made an unlikely pair, with Georgios feeding off Andrew's local glamour and Andrew, in turn, soaking up his friend's passion for pop music.

Georgios had, by this time, wisely dismissed the dismal mid-1970s pop charts as unutterably naff and had started to concentrate on more mature artists, particularly – and portentously – Elton John and Queen (Lesley Panayiotou was thoroughly addicted to Queen, and Bohemian Rhapsody was often played on the household stereo). Andrew warmed to this theme and together the pair would spend hours dissecting the more serious chart records, viciously slagging the naff, wrinkly, 'fag end of glam' artists and discovering the larger picture, the sense and shape of pop, rock and soul.

Although, at this point, Andrew Ridgeley was completely non-musical, his ferocious, if unlikely desire for fame was forged in these sessions. Andrew's endless banter, his evident self-confidence and his all-too-obvious lust for the lighter side of life – girls, pop, football, parties – did not necessarily endear him to Lesley Panayiotou who, perhaps naturally, regarded him as something of an undesirable influence on her son.

She didn't dislike him: indeed, Andrew's natural charm had, in effect, won her over, but that was part of the problem. And nobody could doubt that her fears were well founded. Andrew seemed to be steering a fast course towards teen hedonism, while Georgios still had a deeper side. His love of rock had failed to tear him away from his violin lessons and, when Bushey Meads opened a rather austere new music section, he took full advantage of it, studying music theory up to A-level.

Still, despite Andrew's laddish bent, one has to look hard to find that essential spark of rebellion in the teen years of either boy. In 1976, as most future pop stars were kicked into action by the thrust of blinding white light known as punk rock, Georgios remained soberly unmoved. Perhaps he was merely a little too young to be affected by this new outburst. Later he would state that, although he understood why punk was

a good thing for the music scene in general, he didn't feel it was particularly relevant to him, a young, middle-class rock fan with a growing soul awareness. Little did he know that many of the protagonists of punk, in particular the Bromley contingent, were not only from similar, middle-class backgrounds but were also regulars at the south London soul clubs (many of the 1976 punk fashions, including mohair jumpers, were taken directly from the soul scene).

In any case, the initial impact of punk, although undoubtedly revolutionary within the confines of the music industry, has often been overstated. While a couple of hundred kids here and there might travel to see the Buzzcocks, the youth of Britain, from Brighton to Aberdeen, were cramming into their local nightspots. This was the era not of punk, but of disco.

This was certainly the case with Georgios, who still felt that he had 'nothing to rebel against', preferring to explore his own sexuality and sense of teenage excitement. More cars 'n' girls than drugs 'n' booze, his local Mecca proved to be the disco in Harrow. These weekly under-age forays were most often led by the trendier, more streetwise and cocksure Andrew. Nevertheless, together in mid-teendom, they sneaked past the bouncers and threw themselves with considerable gusto, and a growing athleticism, into their dance-floor antics. Together Georgios and Andrew became soul boys.

Girls, of course, always lurked in the background – although, compared to Andrew, Georgios felt awkward in their presence, wholly unable to instigate chatter or hold their attention. With admiration tinged with envy, he would gaze shyly at the magnetic Andrew, whose charisma effortlessly dominated most evenings.

Nevertheless, by October 1977, he noticed that a girl from Bushey Meads had started to pay him particular attention, hanging adoringly around him in the street and choosing his shoulder to cry on at the occasional 'cider party'. The snogging that naturally ensued would be enough to establish her as Georgios' first real date and together they smooched clumsily on the Harrow dancefloor.

Significantly, after dating for four weeks, Georgios bought her a copy of Chic's Dance, Dance, Dance, which was altogether a more fitting soundtrack to his lifestyle than the Sex Pistol's Pretty Vacant. Although the relationship would fizzle into mutual boredom before the eighth week was out, this period saw Georgios taking more and more interest in his appearance, zipping down to check out the shops of Watford and even, on occasion, London's West End, where he purchased colourful post-soul shirts and peg-topped trousers. At the time he was, or thought he was, just about the ultimate in north-London teen cool. In truth, he was still aspiring to match Andrew's dishearteningly natural trendiness.

This, at least, was his close, if unreachable goal, for Georgios was still dogged by the usual teenage hang-ups. He had finally managed to replace his thick-rimmed glasses with contact lenses – a major breakthrough – but he still suffered (unlike the smooth-skinned Andrew) from bouts of confidence-crushing acne.

Still, the magic of a pop-and-soul teen life surrounded him and, week in week out, Georgios found himself in some darkened suburban living room clutching a girl, as the surrounding revellers melted down to just a few stragglers. Experimenting with alcohol, he seemed to be eternally hovering around that dangerous nausea level that blights all teenage intoxication. Famously, Georgios once vomited all over his much-prized bright green soul trousers. This unfortunate occurrence preceded an intense hour in which he poured out all his teenage trauma – 'I'm ugly, nobody ever fancies me' – to a startled and somewhat irritable Andrew.

In a sense, this outburst highlighted the gulf that still existed between the two boys in terms of self-confidence, for Andrew had little time for pouring out his heart. His vision was still fixed – and certainly not on schooling. Andrew wanted girls, more girls and, perhaps, some kind of musically orientated fame. It was, of course, a stupidly naive and distant ambition but, nevertheless, he persevered with his dreams, forever attempting to nudge Georgios away from his – as Andrew saw it – rather dull academic determination. 'Yog,' Andrew would say – for that had become Georgios' inelegant nickname – 'We are going to make it somehow. I know it.' It was an empty prophesy, for Andrew had no real musical leanings at this point. Ironically, his only hope lay in his friend's dogged pursuit of musical qualifications.

In 1979, just at the point when Georgios was buckling down to his studies at Bushey Meads, Andrew, now post-O-levels, was departing the school for the looser, more appealing regime of a part-time A-level course at nearby Cassio College, which seemed, again to Georgios' chagrin, gloriously mature. Needless to say, Andrew's self-discipline, barely noticeable to begin with, would soon be in tatters. Andrew was to fall, bright-eyed and all too willing, into the unholy camaraderie of the college common room.

2 the young executives

A strand of musical interest still united Georgios and Andrew. 1979 saw the emergence of the Coventry-dominated Two-Tone ska revival, led by the boyish swagger of the Specials and, from London, Madness. Here, at last, was a spirit of rebellion that appealed to them both, for the ska bands married their punky sensibilities with the sounds that had swirled evocatively around skinhead-filled dancefloors ten years previously. Unlike punk, this was a scene that, fashion-wise, melted neatly into society. Their smart, moddish appearance appealed hugely to Georgios and Andrew and immediately, they began planning and then formed their own ska band, the Executive. The speed in which this shameless Specials copy-cat outfit became a local reality is legendary, thanks to a couple of latterday 'I was in George Michael's band' tabloid splashes. Within hours they had recruited two schoolmates, Andrew Leaver and David Mortimer, and twenty minutes later, had dragged in Andrew's younger brother, Paul, to take up the still-vacant position behind the drums.

Somehow, this punkish, amateurish gaggle managed to mould a short, cacophonous, intensely derivative set comprising a huddle of indistinct three-chord sub-ska dirges. During the following weeks, the line-up would fluctuate, with Tony Bywaters and Jamie Gould adding occasional musical weight, and a date for their debut appearance – a bonfire party at Bushey Meads School Scout hut – was tentatively agreed.

It wasn't a difficult debut. Most of the audience, having never seen a 'genuine live pop group' merely stared in awe as the Executive bumbled through their set, with vocalist Georgios adapting his soul dance steps for the stage, and Andrew plodding through bass lines. Both

Georgios and Andrew became instantly hooked on this – admittedly embarrassing – parochial sense of glamour. After the gig they pouted and posed at the rear of the hall, feeling for the first time like pop stars and soaking up the admiring smiles of the girls.

This was, however, truly an illusion, and an illusion that faded once the band had screwed up the courage to look beyond their immediate locality. Nevertheless, regular rehearsals did, at least, provide the band members with a sense of purpose, even if their all-too-swiftly, all-too-muddily recorded demo tape was returned by wholly uninterested record companies (including the Beat's Go Feet Records, who saw 'nothing of any interest or originality' in the recordings). After a few weeks of this, Andrew, who was adopting a new set of college friends, began, in Georgios' view, 'to act pretentiously'. Andrew, while enjoying the warm rush of extremely localised stardom, was also rather taken with the new-found sophistication his college environment provided. Georgios resented this and formed a musical partnership with another, more studious friend, David Mortimer. Reports suggest that it was this duo, rather than Georgios and Andrew, who embarked on courageous and reasonably lucrative busking exploits in the streets and tube stations of north London.

It was during this period that Andrew's noted and tempestuous affair with Shirlie Holliman began. Holliman – beautiful, blonde, a year older and several years ahead of him in terms of sophistication – had initially, and then repeatedly, dismissed the bumbling attentions of Georgios and Andrew as little more than the distant infatuations of 'a couple of kids' – the word 'kids' being, perhaps, the ultimate insult for anyone surging towards their late teens. Holliman had even, on one occasion, ridiculed Georgios in public as he emerged from the school, violin case clasped under his left arm. As for Andrew, she glided serenely away from his vociferous, precocious attempts to impress her – until, that is, she encountered him in a local pub and was strangely drawn to his much-improved social skills. Perhaps, also, her judgement had been affected by the overblown rumours of Andrew's impending pop stardom.

She liked the idea of the band, of being part of something, and before she knew it, she found herself drawn into their inner circle. This wasn't a difficult manoeuvre as, quite obviously, the entire band 'fancied her like mad'. Also, it must be noted, the band rather liked the fact that she held a driving licence. Hence, Shirlie Holliman's first task in the music business was to drive a dreadful ska band to a series of downbeat venues. Somewhere, within all this, and within the numerous band meetings during which swollen egos would clash messily, a germ of originality must have been sown. Georgios Panayiotou began writing songs, to little fanfare at first, as nobody took the slightest notice.

By now, the band was chasing shadows anyway. Their musical vision was falling further and further behind the times. By 1980, the ska revival had all but fizzled out as both the Specials and Madness had managed to find distinctive sounds of their own that would carry them on to a higher level. Mere revivalism was no longer good enough.

Despite this, it was Andrew Ridgeley, still driven by notions of stardom, who managed to kick-start some kind of record-business action. It isn't difficult to understand why his attention

Michael

had, in recent weeks, been grasped by the local mystique of one Mark Dean, who had, in the space of a couple of years, evolved from being Andrew's older, rather bullish neighbour (he was three years Andrew's senior and lived at 25 Chiltern Road, three doors away) to 'that kid who works in the music business'. Although this alone would have been enough to gain Dean a decent measure of 'girl-pulling' notoriety, the truth was unfolding in a rather more unlikely fashion. Mark Dean's first step into the music industry was with a publishing administration company called 'And Son' which, among other things, handled the complex affairs of the Jam. In his capacity as a smart, Moddish junior exec, he proved extremely useful in looking after Secret Affair, whose chart success, although in retrospect a brief flicker, seemed like a big deal at the time. The fashionable, alert, hip young Dean proved to be the perfect link between artist and company.

Within two years, Dean had moved to an A&R post at Phonogram. By sheer force of vision, talent and luck, he helped transform an ailing beast of a record label into an enviably sharp talent-scouting organisation. Dean defied the odds to become the most precociously successful, admired and respected young A&R man in Britain. It was Dean who had the vision to pull the celebrated Some Bizarre album – which contained the likes of Soft Cell, Depeche Mode and Blancmange – onto the flagship Phonogram label. This, of course, meant that he had to deal with the awkwardly eccentric Some Bizarre boss and Soft Cell manager, Stevo, whose flamboyant antics had already caused a number of older Phonogram scouts to run for cover. But Stevo, while cold-shouldering everyone else in the company, warmed to Dean's unconventional

anti-suit approach. Through this association, Dean signed Soft Cell to Phonogram, swiftly followed by perhaps the most critically acclaimed pop band of the 1980s, Sheffield's ABC. It was a remarkable coup and, largely thanks to Mark Dean, Phonogram's street image brightened considerably. They attained a great degree of essential 'hipness'.

All this was in the near future, however, as Andrew Ridgeley passed an Executive demo tape across to a nonplussed Mark Dean, who sat, quietly sipping bitter, in the Three Crowns pub in Bushey. Just one half-hearted listen to the tape convinced him – the Executive were going nowhere. It was cast aside onto Dean's growing pile of 'idiot tapes', a mass of largely uninspired dross that was sent to him from all corners of Britain. There may have been exceptions but, as Dean would later refer to the Executive demo as 'shit', this wasn't among them.

There was now a growing feeling of disillusionment and general apathy within the loose ranks of the band. As Andrew wandered, back and forth, past Dean's house, and watched the silent telephone, and saw the postman neglect to bring good tidings morning after morning, the band was simply falling apart. Andrew, his objectivity completely blown apart, couldn't believe that Dean would not respond. Still, nothing happened and, in the autumn of 1980, just forty-eight hours before the Executive were due to perform at a local college, the band simply walked out following a particularly 'ploddy' rehearsal, leaving Georgios and Andrew to perform the gig as a clumsy duo, with Andrew trying to enliven the proceedings with a curious and, perhaps, unwise burst of cross-dressing.

The Executive – Georgios and Andrew's first band

'Nothing of any

interest or originality'

Go Feet Records reaction to the Executive

Michael

George

③ going for it!

Still unhappy with the hold that Andrew Ridgeley seemed to have over her son, Lesley Panayiotou began to apply a little matriarchal pressure, suggesting rather strongly that her son should 'stop all that pop-star nonsense and concentrate on schoolwork'. To her surprise, this new hard line had a strange, emboldening effect on Georgios, who suddenly showed a stubborn streak and announced that he would leave school immediately if she prevented him from working on his music. Stunned, Lesley duly backed off. Perhaps this was the first time that she realised the true level of her son's commitment. Not, it must be noted, that there was much tangible evidence of this. The band was gone, their efforts as a flamboyant live duo had faded and now they seemed content to carry on their craft in their bedrooms, risking ridicule by announcing to their parents and friends that they were 'concentrating

on their songwriting'.

Nobody was convinced by this. By 1981 Andrew had signed on the dole while Georgios, perhaps as a reflection of his father's work ethic, readily snapped up a flow of mundane part-time jobs from cinema usher to somewhat ignored DJ at a local leisure centre. Both sets of parents were unhappy with this situation, as they watched their sons' job opportunities fading rapidly. The unlikelihood of the pair getting work through their music merely served to dismay their parents even further. In Christmas 1981 Andrew, unable to take any more parental pressure, abruptly left home and took the traumatic though liberating step of moving into a suitably bohemian flat in Peckham, south London, a world away from the comforts of Bushey. Too far away, in fact, for it took just four weeks for Andrew to decide that home life was the easier option: he duly went

back to his parents', humbled though wiser for the experience. A surge of songwriting activity, however, did enliven this spell away. It was in the flat that Georgios and Andrew began discussing the downside and, more interestingly, the merits of dole-queue life. And, as the discussion progressed, it slowly but surely transformed itself into a full-blooded streetwise rap parody, in which a wedge of wordplay was broken up by a daft, bolshy, childish chorus, wrapped around the words 'wham', 'bam' and 'man'. Plucked from that chorus came the title of their new project – Wham! was born.

With loving but unbearable pressure flowing from his parents every breakfast time, Georgios began to instil a greater sense of urgency in his partner, arguing that only sheer hard graft would get them out of their steadily worsening predicament. Both knew full well that they wouldn't be able to continue their quest for pop stardom for long. Something would soon snap – their parents' tempers, probably – and they would be forced to drift back onto rather more mundane career paths. In Georgios' bedroom, with a microphone taped to the top of a broom handle and the accompaniment of a jerky and disturbed four-track recording machine, their endeavours were given an added urgency by the fact that Lesley kept bobbing her head around the door, asking motherly questions and offering endless cups of coffee. Still, the duo managed to record snippets of four songs – Come On, Careless Whisper, Wham! Rap and Club Tropicana. Though raggedly constructed and muffled by the unwelcome impurities of such a low-budget recording, they still managed to contain a surprising degree of vivacity. This nicely rounded quartet of songs stretched far beyond the derivative sub-Two-Tone nature of the Executive's recording, and seemed to mirror effectively the soul-boy lifestyle that they had been attempting to emulate in recent years. Excitedly whisking the tape off to the usual record companies, they were, once again, dismayed to find rejection slips drifting slowly back to them (EMI suggested that they should spend some time on their songwriting, which it described as 'naive'). Dismayed, they approached Mark Dean once again.

By this time, Dean's astonishing rise had thrown him into an intriguing situation. His success at Phonogram had caused a number of record companies to head-hunt him. Warner Brothers led the list, and Dean had started to drift towards their offer when CBS weighed in with an enthusiasm he found difficult to refuse. The ferocity of these offers intrigued him and,

displaying a wisdom associated with businessmen twice his age, he abruptly backed off, delighted to discover that his nonchalance merely served to fan the flames. During his brief rise, Dean had watched how others had manipulated this mentality. In a sense, he was no different than the newest, hippest band – the kind of band that every label needs, if only to supply the illusion that it is at the cutting edge.

Dean, who had been around at the early stages of the vacuous New Romantic scene, had noted how Spandau Ballet, in particular, had milked their own pre-signing hipness by negotiating their own label, Reformation, which was backed by Chrysalis. Similarly, Dean thought that, rather than merely work for CBS, he would prefer to allow them to fund his own label. It was a smart move and, though it would ultimately end in disaster, seemed to cement his reputation.

At the age of 21, he was regarded not only as a particularly alert A&R man blessed with 'great ears', but as a highly astute negotiator. (It wasn't, however, such a mighty deal. Mark Dean's pristine new label, Innervision Records, was expected to flourish on a budget of about £150,000 a year, enough to nurture one act – but Dean had plans for three or four.)

There was, of course, one major flaw here. Mark Dean didn't have an act at all. Indeed, as he settled into his new office, he didn't even have an inkling of where these acts would come from. What happened next was the kind of twist of fate that an open-minded editor might just allow to remain in a work of rock-orientated fiction. Mark Dean wandered home within six weeks of starting negotiations with CBS to find a demo tape lying on his mat. It contained the nucleus of a batch of songs that were to make its singers one of the major forces in the world of pop. This scenario is especially unlikely since the tape was the product of some naive dabbling by two young musicians who lived in his road – musicians whose form to date had been little more than a duff school-hall ska band.

Even Mark Dean, the most precociously successful young A&R man in the country, couldn't possibly be so lucky, could he? Such things just didn't happen. (Interestingly, this writer remembers one notably hapless A&R man from Bronze Records remarking at the time that 'Mark Dean has used up his quota of luck twice over'.) Nevertheless, just one minute after Mark Dean had reluctantly slapped the demo into his tape machine, he knew he had found his first act. Unable to believe his ears, he rewound the tape and played it again, and again, and again. The recording was appalling and the backing equally

Michael

bad, but somehow the songs managed to shine through. Careless Whisper held him spellbound. Wham! Rap was young, fresh, vibrant and surely aimed straight at the charts.

Upon meeting the duo, Dean was surprised to learn that the four songs represented only a small part of their unrecorded repertoire. He wasn't, however, disheartened by the fact that no other company had shown any interest at all, for he was keen to follow his own instincts. Georgios and Andrew displayed extreme naiveté in admitting this to him but they were, naturally, champing at the bit. Terrified of losing the one chance that might come their way, they pushed any kind of business acumen straight to the back of their minds. Wham! wanted to go home and tell their parents that they had secured a recording contract. They wanted to make records. With Dean – equally lost in the dream of his own label, and not wholly sure of the tentative constraints of his contract with CBS – this circle of business naiveté would prove to be a dangerous cocktail indeed. Still, things moved swiftly on. Following a second demo financed by Innervision, contractual negotiations were set in motion. Just one month after completing their bedroom recording, Wham! were virtually signed.

For Georgios in particular, the signing of the Innervision contract and the subsequent legal minefield to which it would lead would prove to be a valuable lesson. In retrospect the contract, which would pay Georgios and Andrew a mere £500 each in recoupable advances, seems almost comical. A letter attached to the contract instructed the boys, quite rightly, to seek legal advice (without it, no contract would be wholly enforceable). As it turned out, they were represented by a regular customer at Jack Panayiotou's restaurant, whose name was Robert Allen. Strangely, this choice wasn't necessarily a poor one for, when the terms of the contract eventually exploded in everyone's face, Allen was swiftly exonerated of any blame. Furthermore, his expertise in music-business contracts was never in doubt.

Certainly, Allen could not be blamed for the farcical situation that surrounded the actual signing of the contracts. Some of the fault lay with Dean's impetuous nature – always keen to get his first act signed and in the studio – and some with his artists, equally keen to 'get this legal stuff over with as quickly as possible'. Problems started when a draft contract was drawn up by Dean's solicitor, Paul Rodwell, which included some, but by no means all, of Allen's amendments. The contract should then have been taken back to Allen for perusal and further negotiation. But Mark Dean, it seems, picked the contract up, mistakenly believing it to be complete and ready to sign. He immediately telephoned the Wham! boys, who were deep in rehearsal at Halligan Band Centre in Holloway and explained that the contracts were awaiting their signature. And so, on 24 March, in a Holloway café, Wham! and Mark Dean signed the deal which would, in time, be referred to whenever music-business schooling took place.

Within the music-law profession it would be seen as one of the all-time-classic contractual gaffes. After all that has been written, one can reasonably assume that all three signatories were convinced they were signing the final and amended document. The fact that the contract wasn't fully prepared would cause the eventual court case to swing firmly in Wham!'s favour.

The boys were delirious. How could they have

'Stop all that pop-star nonsense and concentrate on schoolwork'

Lesley (Georgios mum)

known that they had signed such a crippling document? And it was crippling, too. Despite the fact that some of Allen's amendments did make it into their final version of the contract – for instance, that the boys no longer had to cover the cost of hiring a producer, which had been an absurd idea, to say the least – it remained packed with 'negatives'.

One of these was the severity of Innervision's offer of a mere 8 per cent royalty rate on singles and albums. Furthermore, the contract stipulated that Wham! might have to produce one album per year – with an added album if the company demanded – for four years. Added to this was the insane clause that should the duo split, Innervision would be able to command ten albums from each of the boys. One can sympathise with all parties at this point. As stated, at the heart of this contract were three young boys desperate to get things moving and it wasn't surprising if such blurry contractual

matters could be pushed aside as the lust to climb onto the chart ladder took control. But Georgios, a DJ after all, should have noticed that the contract offered no royalties for sales of 12-inch singles. Not one penny.

To this day, there still exists a mist of uncertainty over the signing. Did Mark Dean really think the contracts were ready? Why did Georgios and Andrew leap into the deal so eagerly? In Johnny Rogan's 1987 book, Wham!: The Death Of A Supergroup, Mark Dean explained the situation in this way: 'George Michael knew that I was probably the best person for the job. He knew that I was going to get the backing and he also knew that I was going to break him before I broke anybody else. He also knew I was completely in love with his music. It was a perfect partnership. But the way we signed – we should never have signed that way. That's the honest truth. We both made a mistake. A classic mistake. We were both very stupid. I shouldn't have approached the matter that way and neither should he. It should have been done properly through the lawyers.'

Not surprisingly, Robert Allen was stunned by the fact that the eagerness of his clients had caused them to forget to consult him before signing. Apparently, he immediately penned a severe letter to Georgios informing him of the unwise nature of his impetuous behaviour. Rather curiously, Allen then also wrote a letter to Innervision, confirming that the contracts that had been signed were binding. How strange. One might expect a letter stating the very opposite. But Allen, clearly, was worried that Georgios and Andrew had ruined the deal, and that Innervision might be tempted to back out.

4 Wham! rap

On an artistic rather than a business level Wham! were gathering momentum. Wisely, they had dropped the notion of working live as a band and instead opted for the easier, modern method of making regular personal appearances at local nightclubs. In an instant, they had dispensed with the deadening logistics of touring with a full-sized band. This way they could flit about and reach the largest audiences with the least amount of technical hassle. They weren't, by any means, the first to adopt this method – PAs were more often than not the simplest way to showcase a featherweight disco or dance act. That Wham! opted for this method – dancing to a 12-inch white label – is, perhaps, indicative of Georgios and Andrew's deep understanding of nightclub mentality. Deep down they were still soul boys, and soul boys wanted to dance. They wanted quick and easy glamour and couldn't have cared

less about the bass player's politics or the drummer's hedonistic bent. Wham!, it was decided, would be a modern pop unit. They would milk dancefloor fervour.

To do this, however, they desperately needed to produce striking, magnetic visuals. They needed females. It didn't take long for Georgios, as official Wham! choreographer, to put Shirlie Holliman into the routine, a role she greedily accepted. As Shirlie danced regularly with her dollybird friend Amanda Washburn, it didn't take long to complete the foursome. By all accounts the rehearsals were hilarious, with Georgios adopting a Travolta-like stance, flipping wildly across the practice room floor and stripping himself of the last of his unwanted puppy fat. These rehearsals were, for Andrew and probably for the two girls as well, something of an eye-opener. Here, for the first time, the furious,

'Deep down they were soul boys'

George

dogged ambition of Georgios Panayiotou was openly exposed. Shedding his unsaleable Greek name he took total control, fuelled with a new-found confidence. He changed overnight. Nothing, now, would stand in his way, Nothing, in George Michael's eyes, could be allowed to halt the progress of Wham!, and he believed that the three other members of the band were similarly fired up.

Imagine, then, his surprise when, on the day that Wham! were to perform in front of a swiftly assembled audience comprising CBS executives (none of whom knew anything about the band other than that they were Dean's first), the hapless 16-year-old Washburn opted out of the performance as she was needed by a close friend to help out in a court case. George couldn't understand this at all and immediately instructed Holliman to tell her that her services were no longer needed. Amanda Washburn's abrupt departure from Wham! was coloured by her understandable indignation and hurt, a feeling that would surely have grown as the band attained success. Her replacement was a part-time model/sales assistant/backing singer called Diane Sealey who despite her various vocational threads, had never been seriously burdened by ambition. Wham! would take her towards fleeting pop stardom. Before she sang a note for them, she decided to change her name to DC Lee.

The initial recording sessions proved promising but as acceptable chart pop had to be given a heavy studio gloss by distinctive producers such as Trevor Horn, it was deemed necessary to search out a suitably 'chart-tuned' producer. George's initial choice was Bob Seargent, already known for his precision work with Haircut 100 and the Beat. But Seargent was keen to return to working on a less obviously pop-orientated project and, much to George's chagrin, he turned them down.

Wham! finally struck a deal with Bob Carter, who had impressed George, if nobody else, with his lush work on the jazz-funk scene, crafting the songs of David Grant's Lynx as well as Light of the World, Beggar and Co and Junior. Overseen by the studious Carter, Wham! Rap was duly moulded into a chart possibility. By the time it had reached the ears of the CBS executives, it had lost a couple of rebellious touches. No longer, for instance, would George Michael punkily bellow: 'You don't take no shit from the benefit', which was a great shame. Despite this, everyone involved seemed content that the vivacious, tempestuous, mildly subversive Wham! Rap would make a perfect debut single.

April 1982

It is indicative of Mark Dean's spirit and resolve that at the precise moment Wham! Rap was let loose on a wholly unsuspecting world, he resolutely refused to seal himself within the little empire of Innervision and devote himself solely to the already problematic career path of his proud new artists. Instead Dean, perhaps addicted to the chase, continued to trundle up and down the motorways of Britain on quests that would invariably see him standing in the darkened shadows of some terrible downbeat venue, fending off overenthusiastic advances from would-be managers while an uninspired drone poured forth from the stage.

Indeed, it would have been far easier for Dean to scrutinise the reports of talent-scouting flunkies, or merely keep an ear tuned to the A&R grapevine. But an A&R rarity, he wasn't that lazy, nor was he afraid to trust his own judgement.

'I don't think I'll ever become part of the A&R pack in that sense,' he stated, before adding, 'in fact, I'm determined not to. It doesn't work for me. I've got to discover something for myself rather than just outbidding someone else.'

These somewhat defiant words were related to yours truly after Dean, in considerable pain from his plaster-clad broken arm, travelled to the parochial outpost of Disley, Cheshire, to sit through a painfully lacklustre rehearsal from a pop parody called the Secret Seven, whose demo, at least, had stirred something in him. After sauntering into the Disley pub and deflecting the intimidating glances from the locals – 'It's like the pub in American Werewolf In London, this, innit?' – he concluded: 'Still, what are they going to do, hit me with me plaster cast?'

At this meeting, somebody presented him with that week's copy of Smash Hits, which included a tiny and wholly dismissive review of Wham! Rap. Clearly disturbed, he launched into a speedily indignant defence of both his label and his artists. 'Innervision is the best way to go,' he stated, not without a certain degree of vocal force, 'and Wham! are not a hype. People think they are at the moment but I'm telling you, they are the biggest thing I have ever been involved in. Something substantial will happen to them. I've lived with the songs for months now. There is a major world talent within Wham!. I know it sounds unlikely, and CBS don't know it yet, but it's there all right.'

It was a curious and, for the assembled Stockport gathering, rather unsettling outburst. But Dean was obviously a man wholly committed, and, as it would turn out, ironically convinced that Innervision and Wham! were both on course for greatness. He was still talking about

Michael

this two hours later as he wandered, dazed, into a local police station after witnessing a particularly horrific motor accident. 'Yes, yes, the car in front of us rolled over,' he informed the policeman matter-of-factly before turning towards us and continuing: 'But Wham! will be big, I'm telling you.'

Initially, neither press, nor radio stations, nor public quite knew what to make of Wham! Rap. The fast, furious and, George Michael would later claim, not overtly serious lyrics could, nevertheless, quite easily be regarded as 'unusually subversive'. After all, here was a song that, rather than bemoaning the miseries of dole-queue life, openly championed the wonders of living off the Giro without a care in the world. Strangely enough, the apparent bravery of this sentiment would gain the band no small number of unlikely Brownie points within the more radical areas of the music press, where journalists, keen to champion lightweight pop that stretched beyond bland sentiment, seemed delighted to stumble upon a genuinely upbeat scream from the British dole queue.

It was a strange period for the still-powerful music weeklies who had, during the previous year, rather neglected their greying 'indie' stance and aligned themselves with the brightness and optimism of out-and-out pop (for a while back there, even Dollar and Bucks Fizz had been considered curiously cool). Wham! Rap, therefore, instantly attained a degree of rather unexpected hipness. Conversely, the song's barbed edges would cause a degree of consternation, most notably at the BBC where, incredible as it may seem now, Wham! Rap managed to evoke a mild but potentially damaging sense of paranoia. After all, this was the post-Falklands War Britain of

1982 and the country, it seemed, was still happy to continue coasting on a tabloid-induced wave of optimism born of the brash, jingoistic hype of the south Atlantic conflict.

And the pop charts, although endlessly intriguing, were filled with the brashness of pastiche. Hadn't Captain Sensible dislodged himself from the ever-darkening grip of the Damned to score a hugely unlikely number one with Happy Talk? Hadn't the ludicrously attired Spandau Ballet forged a direct line between London club life and the upper reaches of the charts? As New Romantics regularly captured the headlines, flouting, pouting and pouncing on paparazzi everywhere, it seemed that Britain was enjoying a second age of glam. And, contrary to the cynical backbiting of the music press in later years, it was fun for a while to be freed from the snarl of the previous decade's punk outburst.

How strange, then, to find Wham! Rap, a single that seemed to straddle both these extremes. But in the NME, George Michael would later claim that people read too much into the track. 'It's not a totally serious song. It's not a matter of us saying that this is what people should be doing. If people take the song too seriously they'll wonder what we are on about because there are a lot of contradictions in there. What we should be doing is educating people on how to deal with it [life on the dole], how to use their leisure time. If you are not able to do anything about it, you might as well have a laugh about it.'

Despite this ripple of interest, however, the song, much to Dean's consternation and Wham!'s increasing frustration, would fail to crack the Top 100. For Dean it was a learning period and forays into Stockport and the like would have to be put on hold for a while. CBS, he decided, was a beast that would take more than a small degree of nudging into action. He was disheartened to realise that his total belief in Wham! wasn't shared by the powers above him. He realised that he would have to promote them himself. But unknown to Dean, or to Wham!, or, for that matter, to CBS, Wham!'s future had already taken an upturn when up-and-coming rock manager Jazz Summers had wandered into the offices of Island music and, by chance, heard a tape of Wham! Rap. 'It just knocked me out. I thought it was so full of vitality,' he later told this writer. 'I think I actually went out and bought it a week later. It seemed obvious that something would happen but, well, no one else was taking any notice. It was a situation that intrigued me even though I didn't know any of the people involved. Only once or twice in a career do you come across this kind of imbalance. It astonished me to see the record doing nothing.'

It did, in truth, cause a ripple in the clubs, but little more. In the north of England, where the single actually attained reasonable sales – presumably because the pro-dole-queue sentiment was a little more marketable in Chorlton-cum-Hardy than it was in Chelmsford – Wham! Rap briefly found itself the subject of a raucous dance, in which girls would be permitted to grasp any loose male who took their fancy. Perhaps mercifully, this never managed to seriously permeate the London clubs, although George and Andrew were delighted to find themselves dancing – less brazenly, one presumes – to the record at the fashionable Camden Palace and Blitz. London clublife was, George and Andrew felt, the centre of everything. It was the energy source, the nucleus. Surface in those surroundings, among those people, and things would happen.

But it was rather more complex than that. Wham! Rap, although selling moderately well, had failed to set the all-important tongues of CBS wagging. In short, the company had decided not to invest huge amounts in the promotion of the group. Dean, naturally, thundered against their indifference while, simultaneously fending off the increasingly frustrated George Michael. It was a no-win situation for the Innervision boss, whose youthfulness suddenly seemed to be a hindrance on both counts. The situation was tricky. At one point, for a full month, Mark Dean and George refused to speak to each other, leaving Andrew Ridgeley looking on in a state of sheer helplessness. Wham! were crumbling after just one release. Unhappy with CBS, Dean took it upon himself to employ a particularly sharp record-plugger – named Bullet – to help push the second single, Young Guns (Go For It), into the public eye. It was an inspired move and, to this day, Mark Dean believes that if Bullet hadn't, literally, 'screamed' the record onto various TV shows, Wham! would have swiftly folded. As it turned out, Young Guns, following a slight hiccup on its second week of release, forged a path to No 3 in the charts. An unforgettable and ferocious Top Of The Pops dance routine clinched it. Wham! were pop stars.

Young Guns was bold, brash, laddish and vibrant, and its core sentiment was a statement of male independence: go out, get drunk, don't get tied down by girls. For the second time, Wham! had produced a single that effectively, and in a mildly subversive manner, mirrored their clubbing lifestyle. Sensing that something interesting might be happening at last, the NME made the

'There is a major world talent within Wham!... CBS don't know it yet, but it's there all right.'

Phonogram A&R man

record its single of the week. Just three months later, a remix of Wham! Rap would also finally puncture the Top 10 and everyone on the tiny Innervision ship would be content.

However, fending off a regular flow of interest from predatory rock managers, Mark Dean should, perhaps, have heeded the warning signs. For something was about to change. He had helped to create an act that was too big, surely, for his delicately placed label to be able to handle for too long. Furthermore, his position as ersatz Wham! manager was in seriously jeopardy. Big money was lurking and the aforementioned vultures were hovering with increasing menace.

George

Jazz Summers (his real name – he was the son of a jazz musician) had spent most of his youth battling against the suppression of army life. He emerged as an embittered 24-year-old, fired by a determination to somehow break into the music business. During a spell working as a radiographer at North Middlesex Hospital, Summers began to flirt, modestly, with music management, pushing a series of small-time bands onto the London pub circuit and taking up managerial duties for the unlikely folk singer-cum-comic Richard Digance.

Following the punk explosion, Summers' activities had tended to misfire as he offered guidance to a variety of uninspired pub-rock acts, all attempting to gain a foothold in the post-punk, new-wave swell of minor chart bands. These failures were soon offset by his involvement with the student band Danse Society and the poppy Blue Zoo. The latter at least crept into the Top 20 with the forgettable Cry Boy Cry; the hit – which entered the charts in the same week as Young Guns – provided Summers with a new found kudos and, for that matter, confidence. With this record under his belt he visited a nonplussed Mark Dean who wasn't overimpressed with Summers' meagre credentials. His determination, which would become infamous in later years following his nurturing of the talented Lisa Stansfield, was not dented, and he visited Wham! publishers Morrison/Leahy with the same goal in his sights.

Sitting proudly in his office at Big Life Management in 1995, Jazz Summers recalled this second meeting. 'When I think back, I had nothing, really. Nothing going for me at all. One hit and I thought I could take on the world. I was pushing them, trying to get a contact number for

the boys, but they were unmoved. After a while, Bryan Morrison just sighed and informed me that this act was far too big for me, that all the top managers in London were after Wham!. I was a bit indignant, and confused, for I didn't think Wham! were that big. But what I didn't know was that Wham! were breaking in a number of countries. I had only heard two lively rap songs, but these guys had Careless Whisper waiting in the wings. They knew that George Michael was a genius and would need top-flight management. I came away annoyed, but they were right, quite right.'

Cleverly, Summers approached the flamboyant Simon Napier-Bell, whose reputation as a pop Svengali had been forged in the 1960s and 1970s, when his hedonistic lifestyle captured the public's imagination and led a new breed of 'artistic' rock management. Never before,

however, had he been confronted by anyone with the sheer fiery audacity of Summers, a one-hit wonder who was sitting in his office virtually demanding that Napier-Bell should enlist him as a partner. Though he was initially offended by Summers' gusto, Napier-Bell's interest was aroused by the mention of Wham!, the very act that had recently captured his imagination as he sat at home entranced by the Top Of The Pops run-through of Young Guns. So incredibly, Simon Napier-Bell and Jazz Summers immediately began working together. Uppermost in their minds was the desire to secure the management contract for the most exciting act in the country – Wham!.

Their dizzying rush of pop stardom didn't prevent Wham! from performing rather smugly at a Christmas charity concert at Bushey Meads School where, naturally, their status had attained god-like proportions offset, no doubt, by savage ripples of schoolyard envy. As such, 1982 closed in triumphant fashion, with George and Andrew lapping up the accolades and, perhaps for the last time, falling about in a state of mind-numbing inebriation on the streets of Bushey. Within three weeks, however, they found themselves for the first time in America, courted by smiling sycophants who tried to guide them this way and that. The powerful team of Freddie De Man and Ron Weisner, the managerial fuel behind Madonna and Michael Jackson, had sniffed the

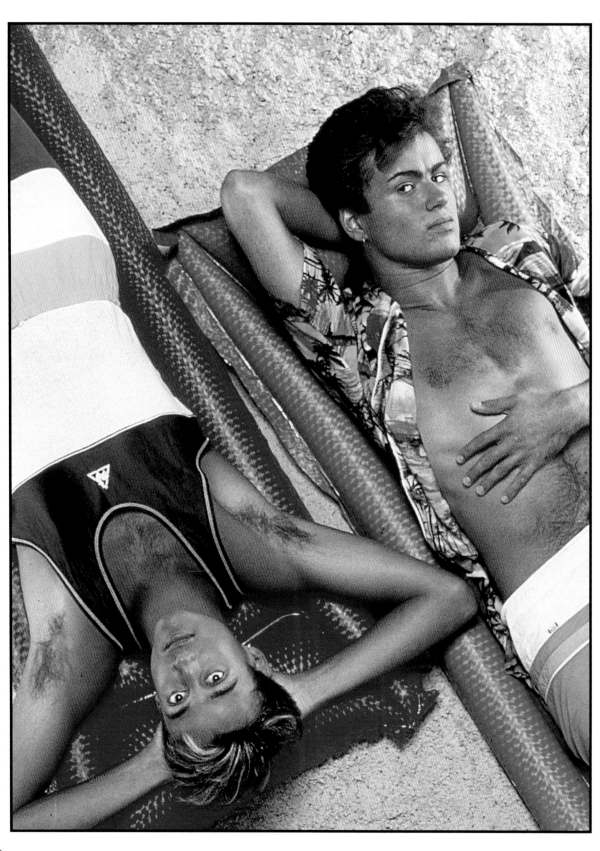

sweet smell of impending global success and offered their services. But it was George, perhaps a little afraid of the high altitude, who decided to reject that particular offer and chose to hide, if only for a short while, behind the part-time managerial double act of Mark Dean and their solicitor, Robert Allen. Hardly a solid arrangement but strong enough, for a time, to allow Wham! to concentrate on their performance.

Wham!'s third and final soul-boy single, Bad Boys – once again a hedonistic, laddish chant – wasn't as effortless or as vital as the first two had been. Perhaps a faint trace of uncertainty had been allowed to seep into the groove, for the recording of Bad Boys was a laboured affair, which spread, expensively, across three separate studios. Uncharacteristically, George had struggled for three months to pin down the rather simplistic theme to a suitable lyrical pattern. Perhaps – and he would later admit this to passing journalists – it was difficult to squeeze another song out of the old soul-and-dole-boy routine, an image that was, in truth, beginning to show signs of cracking (they were never penniless dole boys, anyway). Bad Boys was, if anything, slightly darker than its predecessors, a fact supported by George and Andrew's leather-clad publicity shots. More Gene Vincent than Ricky Nelson, it was a surprising twist in a pop era dominated most tastelessly by young, sockless boys in pastel-coloured trousers. But if the song lacked a certain bite, the George Michael-choreographed dance routine proved sensational and, in May 1983, powered the song to No 3 in the charts.

This was the period that would highlight the differences between the roles and responsibilities of George and Andrew. For Andrew, it was a peak time, that boom period when the intrusive huddle of paparazzi was welcomed, and an appearance at the Camden Palace nightclub would see him revelling in his role as the absolute, unrivalled centre of attention. Although George wasn't unhappy with this degree of interest, his thoughts were commanded by an encroaching terror. Bad Boys had, in a sense, taken the initial Wham! image one step too far, and it didn't take a PR genius to realise that these two immensely photogenic boys might soon find themselves trapped in a particularly unforgiving pop cul-de-sac. The worry was genuine and the chances were, frankly, that the hyperbole might burn out before the true scope of George's rapidly improving songwriting was allowed to reach the surface. With this in mind, the writing and recording of the first Wham! album seemed loaded with dangers.

There were other, more pressing problems, too. It had naturally started to dawn on the boys that, despite their runaway success and fantastically high profile, they didn't, physically, have any money to hand. The problem was that obvious. Ironically, the point when the Wham!/Innervision relationship truly darkened was the moment Bad Boys shot the band to the forefront of British pop. That precise instant of success served to highlight the huge drawbacks of their recording contract. At this point, George and Andrew stormed into Mark Dean's office, intent on forcing an instant renegotiation, only to be flatly informed that, although it was true that Wham! were suffering from the inevitable cash-flow problems, the Innervision situation was even worse. However, Dean did attempt, on behalf of Innervision and Wham! (his role was becoming a little confused by now) to get CBS to renegotiate

Michael

the overall contract. Things had changed. Wham! were looking set to become long-term hit artists and, frankly, the contract simply wasn't adequate.

It was an absurd scenario. All the dreams of both label and band had come true and yet both had been pitched into a nightmare. However, at the back of George's mind lurked one precious thought. He was the one person who held the key to the situation. He was the creator. Everything revolved around him. He had three hits behind him and a number of finer songs captured in his notebook, if not on the debut album, the completion of which had exhausted him. But he was the one who wielded the power. With this thought bubbling away, he fled the country and managed to take his mind off the infuriating swirl of pop stardom by stretching out on a Cyprus beach. It was to be the most important holiday of his life. He knew full well that Wham! had surged out of control and that pop stardom, the one thing he had always dreamt of, wasn't quite what he expected. Suddenly, it wasn't fun at all. No longer could he skip down to the nightclubs of London. He couldn't even enter any of his local pubs without attracting derision or overt adoration or both. Obvious trappings but, frankly, it hadn't dawned on him that they would be so difficult to deal with – especially as these problems didn't seem to be softened by a huge injection of cash. And where was all the money going? Would he, at the end of this – and it was still quite possible that Wham! and his career might end abruptly – find himself falling headlong into the arms of the taxman? It didn't seem right. Dean was too young. George knew that Innervision, like Wham!, had impetuously signed themselves into a mess. Only one thing was certain: this needed sorting out. And fast.

Unsure of his next move, he dithered a little on his return, blocking all channels of communication with Innervision and, perhaps more seriously, with Morrison/Leahy who seemed at least able to convince the ailing Robert Allen that Wham! were becoming far too big for him to handle. Despite having to break through George Michael's natural and understandable terror of the high-powered management team, the bullish Nomis duo finally convinced him that if global chart domination was his goal, then there were forces out there, in America, Japan and Europe, that needed expert handling. Robert Allen and Mark Dean were out of their depth. This had become obvious when Dean had started to mull over the idea of a major tour to coincide with the release of the album. Suddenly it had dawned on him that such a tour needed adequate financing and, frankly, he had no idea how to achieve this. By contrast Simon Napier-Bell, once ensconced in his 15 per cent management chair, would waste no time at all in securing a £50,000 licensing deal with the newly hip Fila sportswear company. The money would be used to underwrite the tour. It was simple, effective and, even George had to admit, achingly obvious.

As Jazz Summers put it: 'To be honest, and I can be honest now, I couldn't believe my luck. Suddenly I was part of Nomis and co-manager of the act I had wanted ever since I had heard that demo tape. It was all too much, tremendously exciting because I knew, by now, that George Michael was a genius. We were prepared to work on a three-month-contract basis. We were on 15 per cent. It was a good deal for them and, because we knew they would be fantastically successful, it was a good deal for us.'

Commercially, everything appeared serene. The

Michael

band's fourth single, Club Tropicana – a noticeably softer, summery affair than the earlier hits which caused many a previously sympathetic critic to immediately jump ship – lodged itself effortlessly in the Top 5 while the debut album, Fantastic, surprised nobody by perching itself on the top spot. However, despite being heartily championed by the influential journalist Dave McCullouch in the music paper Sounds – thus assuring a small but continuing degree of hipness – and being taken to the hearts of screaming teenagers fresh from their knicker-wetting adventures in Durannie-land, there was still an undeniable emptiness about the album that rather curiously mirrored Frankie Goes to Hollywood's disappointing debut album, Welcome To The Pleasure Dome.

As the needle skipped across the tracks, it became difficult to see just what George Michael had been labouring over during those dark, pre-Nomis months. There were just eight songs on the album, four of them singles and one a somewhat unremarkable cover of the Miracle's frantic dancefloor classic, Love Machine (which, admittedly, added a little weight to a fabulous and famously Fila-garbed appearance on the music programme The Tube). Not that Wham!'s new teen audience complained. From the somewhat smarmy-looking cover smiled the two most handsome faces in pop and that, for a while at least, would be enough to carry the band onto a higher commercial level.

Not everyone was happy, though. The girls had all but receded into insignificance by now and DC Lee, unable to cope with the lack of attention, took the opportunity to leap from the ascendant Wham! to Paul Weller's arguably more stable vehicle, the Style Council. Her replacement

was the voluptuous Pepsi De Manque. She slotted neatly into place and eventually became half of the post-Wham! Pepsi and Shirlie, who had a brief pop career of their own.

Beyond the chart success, however, the dark clouds of litigation were gathering. However exaggerated, stories about George and Andrew, No 1 album artists who still had to return home from London appearances on public transport, did not go down well with Simon Napier-Bell, who immediately placed the blame on the shoulders of Mark Dean. Napier-Bell had little time for Dean's juvenile antics and, despite conciliatory objections from Summers, he began talking to CBS behind Dean's back. From here, the situation rapidly deteriorated for Dean. Napier-Bell replaced Robert Allen with Russell's, Morrison/Leahy's heavyweight music lawyers, and despite CBS's initial resistance to the bullying Napier-Bell, it soon became clear that the Wham!/Innervision relationship was over.

On 7 October 1983, Mark Dean was sitting in his South Molton Street office, mulling over the situation, when a letter arrived. Intriguingly, the envelope was marked, 'Strictly private and confidential: For the attention of Mr Mark Dean and for his eyes only'. A chill ran down his spine as he tore into the envelope. To his astonishment, he cast his eyes over a painstakingly brutal, twenty-four page account of the apparently multitudinous failings of Innervision. The document concluded with the assertion that the contract between the company and Wham! was no longer legally binding. In short, his group had been torn away from him. Stunned, he sat down, placed his head in his hands and, in his words, 'nearly died'.

The author of the letter was never determined.

6 making it big!

Dean reacted in the only possible way – he immediately sought an injunction preventing Wham!, in the short term, from negotiating a contract with any other company. The whole sorry affair tilted into frozen legal waters in November, effectively halting the band's progress for the next three months.

During this time, Mark Dean seized his last opportunity to exploit his rapidly disappearing act and rush-released the Club Fantastic Megamix, a cash-in hotchpotch featuring segued tracks A Ray Of Sunshine, Come On and Love Machine. The disc's frantic pace, however, not only seemed to suit the times but also deflected a few of the 'Wham! to split' rumours that, much to the consternation of all concerned, had started to surface in the press. These rumours were heartily denied by Andrew Ridgeley in Aberdeen at the start of the 31-date Club Fantastic Tour.

The tour was neatly timed. As the legal problems continued to simmer away in London, the band, at least, could rise above such horrors and concentrate on what should have been a celebratory romp around Britain. The show was clever, too. The band dispensed with the notion of a support act and instead, hired Capital Radio DJ Gary Crowley to open the set with his roadshow, re-creating the atmosphere of a disco rather than a straightforward concert at the venue. A certain intimacy was attempted by the courageous use of a slide show, featuring shots from the boys' childhood days. A neat trick indeed, making the girls in the audience feel 'part of something'.

Needless to say, the choreography was spellbinding, with the Fila-clad lads bouncing around in front of the highly glamorous Pepsi and Shirlie who, visually at least, very nearly stole

George and Andrew modelling the t-shirts that became synonymous with the 80s

the show. Naturally perhaps, the fevered adoration of the girls in the stalls was squared by a rapidly hardening music press, who now viewed the band (wrongly) as a typical Napier-Bell exercise in lucrative puppetry. It was nothing of the sort but, in the wake of the distinctly lightweight album and throwaway Megamix, Wham! could hardly have expected to hang on to even a minute degree of hipness in the press.

This was never more obvious than in the pages of Blitz magazine, a brasher alternative to The Face now sadly defunct. Blitz had employed the services of Paul Morley, formerly of the NME and Stockport, who had, without doubt, gone beyond the boundaries of the standard rock interview, using a mixture of pseudo-intellectualism and sheer bloody-minded arrogance to unsettle his subjects. This was a task he seemed born to undertake and many a superstar was suitably, and most entertainingly ridiculed. Now it was time for Wham!.

Morley once told this writer that, 'that Wham! interview was easily the best thing I ever did. They fell into every trap, they stumbled at every simple trick. It must have been the first time that anyone had asked them questions that they had to think about. They weren't expecting it and, although they were both bright and made some excellent points, they didn't seem to realise that I would be the one writing the piece up. Effectively, during the scope of that interview, I was God. They could not win. That was what was so funny because they tried, they really tried, and some of my arguments were absurd. But I controlled the pen.'

The resultant article, which would resurface in Morley's book, Ask: The Chatter Of Pop, was simply stunning – the meeting of overanalytical journalese and the banal hyperbole of a pop band that Morley rather cleverly called W Ham United. Here's a tiny but juicy snippet.

Morley: 'How can you feel in any way satisfied or inspired being a prime part of the current charty gay abandon, all this flimsy, jingly singalong?'
George Michael: 'What fucking right have you got to say that we should sing something that is socially important?'

And that, frankly, serves as a reasonably adequate microcosm of an article that, to hard-core Blitz readers, would paint Wham! as the ultimate in cynically marketed pop and Morley as the clever-clever hack. How ironic, then, to see the writer, penniless at the time of the interview, merging with pop producer Trevor Horn to form ZTT and impose his new-found cynical marketing expertise on his old friends from the underground Liverpool scene, the aforementioned Frankie Goes to Hollywood.

1984

Mercifully for all concerned, the crippling litigation process halted on 23 March 1984, with Mark Dean settling for a reasonable pay off that even included a small stake in future Wham! recordings. This was not bad, but he knew only too well that the chance of holding a globally successful act had slipped away from him.
Later, in Johnny Rogan's Wham!: Death Of A Supergroup, Dean would swing over to the philosophical side of things. 'I came out with almost nothing, but as a person, today, I can sit here with no fear, no worry. I'm happy with myself and I'm going to go on and do great things.' Defensive bravado? Feeble consolation?

'What fucking right have you got to say that we should sing something that is socially important?'

George to Paul Morley in a Blitz magazine interview

Michael

Maybe, but Mark Dean was surely far from comforted when George Michael, in the pages of Time Out magazine, explained: 'In some ways he was very good to us. But somebody would have broken Wham! some day.' Again maybe, maybe not. The fact remains that, as bad as that Innervision contract was, it still put Wham! on the road to stardom. Would someone else have picked up the thread? Who knows? But that story belongs to Mark Dean, who would later decamp to America and a lucrative A&R post with MCA.

With Innervision fading rapidly into the background, Napier-Bell immediately adopted a PR role and began to walk among the press, liberally scattering daft Wham! stories, bolstering their image in print while deliberately pulling them back from the direct glare of television. Much to George and Andrew's sheer delight, the boys became the country's second most sought-after subject for the ravenous paparazzi (after Diana, Princess of Wales, presumably).

Lingering beneath the surface of many of these tabloid reports – Napier-Bell had no time for Morley-style music-press idiocy – were cleverly placed mentions of Wham!'s next single, a sprightly, shameless blast of Motownesque pop, significantly recorded in Pittsburgh, Pennsylvania. Wake Me Up Before You Go Go was a rarity – a featherweight romp given a welcome tinge of black R&B. Had it been recorded in England, it might so easily have been sugar-coated in the Trevor Horn/Dollar style. As it was, Wake Me Up Before You Go Go even managed to defy the odds and capture the musically accolade of Single of the Week in Melody Maker. Not that the legions of Wham! devotees, or Napier-Bell for that matter, could have cared less about that. The song zipped past Duran Duran's Reflex, a bewilderingly pompous slab of surreal pap that was, nevertheless, still adored by teendom.

But with Wake Me Up, the boys were back, all brown-limbed and Fila'd up, exciting the girls in the Top Of The Pops studio. It was a return to form, of sorts, for Wake Me Up, although lacking any trace of social comment – or any trace of any kind of comment, come to think of it – was every bit as vivacious as Wham! Rap. The song simply hurtled from the speakers of home radios and shop tannoys. Although 'serious' music fans would naturally object to the song's lack of depth, this was no longer a convincing argument. It was just pop music, nothing more or less. And if you didn't like Wake Me Up Before You Go Go, you didn't really like pop music. Ironically, it was Paul Morley's pet popsters, Frankie Goes to Hollywood, who, two songs into an incredible, record-breaking run of just three mighty hit singles, would finally replace Wake Me Up in the top spot with their hilarious Two Tribes, a dull song enlivened by Horn's scorching production and Morley's surrounding hyperbole. As if part of a logical continuation of the Morley/Wham! spat, the two songs seemed quite the antithesis of each other, with Wake Me Up opting for a clear, lively, joyously meaningless trip and Two Tribes attempting to convey a message, of sorts, through a simple stretch of pop rhythm.

This intriguing battle continued beyond the songs and onto the surrounding T-shirts and general paraphernalia. Morley's 'Frankie Says' range of slogans briefly saw his pretentious one-liners – 'Arm the unemployed', for instance – spreading across the chests of 1984's teen army, while Wham! fans, mainly girls, would soon be sporting such slogans as 'Choose Wham!' and 'Number One'. Both sets of shirts, shamelessly mirroring the political T-shirt slogan developed by designer Katharine Hamnett, would throw a selection of new buzz words into the playgrounds of Britain. For three full months, bewildered teachers would have to come to terms with bolshy girls returning their questions with the meaningless 'Say Wham?' (1984 teenspeak for 'What did you say, sir?').

The second age of glam was over. Now it was time for big, bold and bolshy. A time to go for it. A time to make it big. George Michael seized the opportunity, in London's Time Out magazine, to explain to journalist Simon Garfield – later to pen an erudite account of Wham's legal problems within the context of his major study of music-business double-dealing, Expensive Habits – that, unlike certain other groups (i.e. Frankie), Wham! were puppets to nobody. They were masters if not of their own destiny, then certainly of their creative output.

This was only partly true, for it had become increasingly obvious, even to the tabloids, that the power of Wham! lay completely in the hands of George Michael. What they didn't know, however, was that his songwriting was swiftly gaining depth and elegance. Wake Me Up had, in effect, wrongfooted Wham!'s most persistent critics, who reasoned that George Michael was drifting in an increasingly lightweight direction. He wasn't. In fact, he was beginning to tap into a rich seam of emotion-stacked melodious songwriting that was, frankly, unparalleled, at least within the confines of the British pop charts. In a taxi ride to the airport, en route to France, where Wham! were going to record their second album, a haunting melody seeped into George's head and a song began to form. Within twenty-four hours, the song had been written, complete with emotive lyrics about a boy, besotted with his girlfriend, attempting to understand quite why her attentions continue to drift towards rival males. In October 1984 the song, Freedom, provided Wham! with their second No 1 single.

Before that, the summer was extensively soundtracked by the lilting beauty of the long-awaited Careless Whisper, George Michael's first solo single and the first time the general public had a chance to appreciate the rolling beauty and staggering potential of his songwriting. The track stretched dreamily across a hot August, offering, among other things, a haunting, sliding saxophone that sexily transformed the song – a tale of whispered, brooding, dangerous secrets – into a lush, all-enveloping sound. How different it seemed from the version of the same song that had graced that initial Wham! demo tape and had been ironically dubbed Tuneless Whisper by George's sister Melanie.

Furthermore, the song did, in the end, carry the proud production credit of George Michael. And this despite the fact that Michael had initially travelled to Muscle Shoals studios, in Alabama, to record the song under the aegis of the legendary soul producer Jerry Wexler.

The trip had been indicative of George's latent desire to lift his music to the level of classic pop – or soul. Although George's trip was made by Wexler informing him that he had 'the nearest thing to a black voice that I have ever heard from a European', he returned unhappy. Eventually, after several more attempts, he took over the production duties himself and astonished everyone by slipping effortlessly into the role, 'playing' the mixing desk like a time-honoured professional. Nothing in George's past had indicated that he might be capable of such high-level orchestration and Careless Whisper, in its final form, proved to be an astonishingly complex tune.

But the song did have a downside. Its emergence at the top of the charts served to intensify the 'Wham! to split' rumours that had been bubbling away all summer, despite consistent denials from both boys. That stated there was, undoubtedly, a widening gulf between them, professionally if not publicly, and it showed clearly in the huge and multitudinous differences between Wake Me Up Before You Go Go and Careless Whisper. While Andrew Ridgeley was still wallowing in the glare of teen-pop stardom, George Michael had long since planned his evolution into the role of a mature pop idol.

Floating Careless Whisper as a solo single before Wham! had ended their natural life was – Summers and Napier-Bell knew full well – an obvious precursor to a more lasting existence as a solo performer. Although George strove to quash such suggestions and publicly stated that Wham! was 'very much an ongoing affair – I love working with Andrew', his career path seemed clearly marked out for him. Undoubtedly, the runaway success of Careless Whisper – George Michael's first classic record – effectively sealed Andrew Ridgeley's fate.

The summer of 1984 was a time of political turbulence and strife, when a resolute Thatcherite government met dogged resistance from the National Union of Mineworkers head on, in the bitterest outbreak of picket-line warfare in British history. Naturally, perhaps, Britain's pop artists swayed heavily onto the side of the miners and, at first, it must have seemed perfectly acceptable for Wham! to follow suit.

Jazz Summers wasted little time in phoning the band, gaining their interest and then saying 'yes' to the NUM, who asked if Wham! would perform at a miners' benefit at the Royal Festival Hall. Their socialist instincts aroused, both men jumped at the chance. While no one ever doubted that their intentions were honourable, as soon as they bounced onstage it became clear that the appearance was a huge PR mistake. They performed before Paul Weller's Style Council – which included DC Lee – a band who had never attempted to hide their socialist leanings. But Wham! were a different matter altogether. Indeed, Wham!'s post-Young Guns image, one of eternal holidaying, all-night clubbing, sports-gear wearing and free spending, tended to reflect a lifestyle somewhat detached from the mining villages near Doncaster.

The denim-clad Style Council fans jeered the Wham! boys and the very next week, the music press followed suit, damning the lads with the charge of committing an act of gross hypocrisy, of establishing a junior Thatcherite image and yet still attempting to pledge allegiance to the miners. Though the criticism was way off the mark, and the boys were stunned by the subsequent bad press, it could have been avoided.

As Jazz Summers said: 'George was really upset by the criticism, although it seemed, from the outside, a bit contradictory, with Wham! flouting their sportswear onstage. It wasn't like that at all. The miners asked them to do it and they genuinely wanted to raise some money to help the cause. But I felt that the audience were a disgrace. Many of them were pseudo-socialists anyway, SWP perhaps, people who thought the whole thing was really trendy. That was the really annoying aspect. They were the ones who were being hypocritical, not Wham!. Wham! made a lot of money for the NUM that night and I didn't see that mentioned by any of the critics. Funnily

enough, the NUM were really grateful. The miners understood and Scargill came backstage with his entourage and thanked the band personally.'

Significantly, when the Red Wedge movement began to draw pop stars to its Labour-supporting heart in 1986, George flatly refused to be associated with it. Once bitten, one might say, and strangely nobody seemed to complain when Spandau Ballet turned up for their Red Wedge stint in their respective Porsches.

Perhaps, then, George felt no guilt when the launch party for Wham!'s second album, the arrogantly titled Make It Big, turned into a £10,000 extravaganza taking place at the glitzy Xenon nightclub and heavily reported the next day in the tabloids. The evening proved to be a veritable paparazzi feast, with a whole string of pop starlets – Spandau Ballet, Duran Duran, Bob Geldof and Paula Yates, not to mention a strange gaggle of ageing stars, including Frankie Howerd, Lulu and Kenny Lynch – dutifully posing for the flashes before neatly filing in.

Maybe the stories and the photographs didn't help to dispel the lingering criticism, but, in truth,

Michael

£10,000 is not a great deal of money to spend when the results prove so instant. Subsequently, Wham! were hailed as the band to be seen with – and all this on the eve of the release of Make It Big. It was a PR dream. Afterwards, nobody could have been in the least bit surprised to see Make It Big race to the top of the album charts where it lingered, mockingly, above Frankie Goes to Hollywood's anti-climactic Welcome To The Pleasure Dome.

Not that Make It Big could have been regarded as a full artistic success, and the critics needed no help in tearing into yet another album that seemed astonishingly lacking in scope (which was the norm, in 1984, when Duran Duran, Culture Club, Frankie Goes to Hollywood and a sorry plethora of second-division stars all failed to establish themselves beyond the realm of the singles act).

To his credit, George had always stated that, initially at least, he wished to work within the confines of the standard pop single – that his latterday work would spread way beyond this self-imposed constraint is another irony. As Wham! never claimed to be anything other than a singles unit, perhaps one can forgive the albums that are largely a collection of singles and would-be singles.

On Make It Big, however, was the mighty Everything She Wants. After Careless Whisper, here was another indication that George Michael, when freed from the rapid-fire hype of the Wham! circus, was capable of becoming a songwriter of depth and elegance. Again, however, the critics missed this example of sublime, emotive songwriting and dismissed Wham! as ever-lighter teen-pop fodder. But the Wham! fans couldn't care less about this, and

'The nearest thing to a black voice that I have ever heard from a European'

Jerry Wexler - producer

Make It Big made the Christmas list of every girl in the country under 16. Perhaps more significantly still, across the Atlantic, Wake Me Up Before You Go Go had, somewhat astonishingly, crawled to the top of the Billboard Top 100 (Careless Whisper, in America credited to George Michael and Wham!, would soon follow).

Back in England, all the expectations were that Wham!'s following single, the glorious love drama Last Christmas – a teasing, lyrical nod back to a previous year's ill-advised sexual encounter, guaranteed to tweak the guilty hearts of a million Christmas revellers – would climb effortlessly to No 1. But it wasn't to be. That spot would belong to something else. Something bigger than anyone could previously have imagined.

Band Aid

Lured by the volcanic enthusiasm of Bob Geldof, George Michael dutifully turned up at Trevor Horn's Sarm West Studios in London to take his place alongside Bono, Sting, Simon Le Bon, Bananarama, Paul Young, Paul Weller and the cream of British pop music. They were each pitching in with a vocal contribution to Band Aid's monumental Do They Know It's Christmas?. Immediately, the standard complaint about British pop music being trivial, juvenile and even on occasion moronic was irrevocably flattened.

The Band Aid single would sell more than seven million copies worldwide, providing nearly £7 million for the Ethiopian appeal as well as alerting previously unaware western eyes to the magnitude of the famine problem. Indeed, Band Aid would unleash a mighty wave of famine-relief activity at the top end of the entertainment industry, a wave that would last several years, until, jaded by one-too-many appeals, apathy would once again settle over the western world. Nevertheless, the fantastic achievements of Band Aid cannot be overstated and the British government should feel ashamed by its refusal to waive the 15 per cent VAT levy on the single. This was an astonishing display of greed that temporarily overshadowed the difficult legal situation surrounding Wham!'s Last Christmas.

By the time it became clear that Band Aid was a runaway success rather than a mere gesture, George Michael had already decided to donate his royalties from the million-selling Last Christmas to the same appeal fund. This magnanimous gesture, which George would repeat time and time again throughout his career, edged into the farcical a couple of months later when Dick James Music instigated proceedings against him. They alleged that George had used a large slice of Barry Manilow's Can't Smile Without You in writing Last Christmas. This effectively froze the Ethiopia-bound donation. Thankfully, common sense eventually prevailed and because of the 'exceptional circumstances', Dick James dropped the action.

George

By February 1985, the growing chasm between Wham! and their closest rivals, Frankie Goes to Hollywood, began to gape to extraordinary proportions. The cleverness of the Frankie hype, which certainly caused a stir in Britain, seemed strangely restrictive abroad, especially in the States, where Morley's snappy slogans carried no weight at all (furthermore, Frankie's mockery of Ronald Reagan in the Two Tribes video failed to arouse the dormant rebellious instincts of America's youth). Wham!, by comparison, were moving rapidly from ubiquitous, saleable, quick-fire pop, to melodious maturity. In either role, they upset nobody and climbed effortlessly onto the massive web of American radio playlists, where they proved hugely accessible. Wham! were also perfectly suited to the all-powerful video vehicle of MTV, where their tanned, sporty, rich-boy image melted gloriously into a vision of the Californian dream. George Michael, perhaps, has much to thank Jazz Summers for in this respect, for it was Summers who, despite his lack of experience, masterminded the US invasion with skill, precision and sheer bloody-minded cheek.

Summers says: 'It was largely common sense. I spent a lot of time chatting to the movers and shakers in America. I had a few strong contacts and I took it from there. Nothing mysterious, nothing overtly clever but it did seem to me that a lot of British acts were failing in the States simply because the management were not willing to play it the American way. I just fell in line with American expectations. I told them that Wham! were the biggest band in the world and they believed me. But the true praise must go to them. I hadn't quite realised it before, but Wham! were producing universal product.'

'Sometimes I just have to pinch myself.
Sometimes I just can't believe it's
getting so big, so big it's scary'

Andrew Ridgeley

Universal product? That realisation was laying heavy on the mind of Napier-Bell, who watched with no small degree of admiration as his partner systematically broke down the myth that British pop acts couldn't conquer America. The right product, he knew, could be sold almost anywhere. He had known this, in fact, from the moment he first saw the band on Top Of The Pops. But, at the back of his mind, a thought had been niggling away for some time. Biggest band in the world... He liked that phrase and seriously believed that Wham! might actually grow to fit it.

But what would the biggest band in the world do? What massive chances would they have to take, along the way in order to raise themselves above the rest of the pack? What, if anything, could Wham! do that hadn't been done before? Napier-Bell's thoughts turned east towards vast, undiscovered, unlikely, unwelcoming – China.

What a coup it would be, he reasoned, if Wham! could be the first major pop act to perform in that country. The idea, clearly, was absurd. For weren't the youth of China labouring under a repressive blanket ban on western pop? On the other hand, he had heard somewhere – on TV probably – that ripples of new liberalism had started to drift across the country, and that the rock-starved youth of China were ready to grasp western pop with unparalleled fervour (they had previously been allowed to taste only the live delights of the ubiquitous Jean-Michel Jarre). Maybe it could happen.

Intrigued, Napier-Bell visited Canton where he was astonished to discover that a Chinese record company had taken advantage of the relaxing of the previously stringent entertainment laws and had started to release terrible pseudo-disco records. With no competition in sight, disco fever had gripped the youth of Canton. (Johnny Rogan's Wham! Death Of A Supergroup reveals that these awful disco albums were notching up sales of over 40,000.) This somewhat comedic situation was, he reasoned, simply perfect for an act like Wham! who, like Jarre, would surely prove ubiquitous enough to be allowed to play. While in Canton, Napier-Bell noticed an English copy of the China Youth Daily, which contained the encouraging statement: 'Play is also a form of production. Only with an adequate amount of wining and dining and fun and games will the productive powers of the workers be restored.'

Napier-Bell loved that. He loved, also, the thought that, in China, there were 200 million people between the all-important ages of 18 and 32. Calculations began swiftly rattling away in his mind. If Wham! could only tap into this market. Despite rubbing up against a formidable degree of stark, unmoveable bureaucracy, he had managed to persuade a delegation of embassy officials to view a Wham! performance in Hong Kong. To his surprise he discovered that, beneath this surface level of bureaucracy existed a layer of bright, cosmopolitan officials, schooled in western universities and not at all opposed to the idea of introducing pop music to their country.

The problems were still many, however. Napier-Bell had to gain the support of the All China Youth Federation for a start, who needed to be persuaded to issue an official invitation for the band to be able to get permission to play. This served to highlight the problems, for the Federation demanded to view Wham! videos and, equally worryingly, asked for a complete translation of the band's lyrics. Napier-Bell had to be extremely careful. Back in his office he duly flicked through Wham!'s collection of videos

with a sinking heart. It didn't look too good. Suddenly the brazen sexuality of Wake Me Up Before You Go Go seemed unforgivably obvious. Young Guns and Wham! Rap both seemed boldly anti-authoritarian, Bad Boys and Club Tropicana were, in this new light, precariously hedonistic, and steamy sex scenes ran the length of Careless Whisper. The only slice of presentable Wham! came in the form of a surprisingly lacklustre Top Of The Pops run-through of Freedom. Even this worried Napier-Bell. Would the sensitive Chinese sense an anarchic undertone to the word? One had to be so careful. Mercifully, the dull Freedom film seemed to be enough to satisfy the suspicious Chinese although, hilariously, they objected to the daft and sexually parodic Love Machine.

After accepting his 'toned down' version of these particular lyrics, the Federation then shocked Napier-Bell by demanding that all the gate receipts be returned to their cause. Every last one! In fact, the final contract was even worse than this. It demanded that Wham!, while receiving no money, actually paid for the hall, the stage, the free programmes and even the stewards' wages. It was outrageous but Napier-Bell, still sensing a major worldwide PR coup as well as the commercial possibilities in China – provided the government didn't cream off all the royalties – simply couldn't resist. He duly bowed to authoritarian greed. It went ahead.

George and Andrew, astonished by their co-manager's supreme vision, were, initially at least, greatly excited by the prospect which seemed certain to earn them a place in rock history. Even George, jaded beyond belief by touring in the States, found that his appetite for playing live instantly returned (he even made a guest

Michael

49

appearance with Frankie Goes to Hollywood at a Birmingham gig, and gained the admiration of the Liverpudlians for his tremendous capacity for drink at the post-gig binge). As for Andrew, busily fending off yet more media rumours about his impending departure from Wham! – and, for that matter, his increasingly frantic West End fun-boy lifestyle – he realised that the Nomis team were suddenly playing for very high stakes indeed. 'Sometimes I just have to pinch myself,' he stated. 'Sometimes I just can't believe it's getting so big, so big it's scary.'

It was, indeed, getting scary. The impending China tour was beckoning, perhaps a little too hard. Two days before they were due to leave, George Michael telephoned Napier-Bell and asked: 'Simon, are you really sure about this?' Napier-Bell's reply was strongly in the affirmative, although we can only speculate on the emotions that were churning beneath his superficial aura of supreme control. On top of the logistical nightmare, expenses were mounting up horribly. Napier-Bell had managed to bring on board the esteemed film director Lindsay Anderson who, like many of his peers, had deviated into the lucrative market of the pop video. Anderson would film the entire tour and wrap up the whole shebang in a film provisionally entitled Wham! In China: A Cultural Revolution. The film caused the total costs to escalate to ludicrous proportions although Napier-Bell kept on telling himself it would later reap a huge return. Selling this idea to George and Andrew proved problematic too, for both of them were worried about the subsequent intrusion (and, as it turned out, their instincts were correct).

Things weren't helped by the fact that neither of the boys had heard of Anderson or seen either of his classic films, If and Oh Lucky Man. Nevertheless, eventually they agreed. A tiny proportion of this cost would be offset by inviting four British newspapers, The Sun, the Mirror, the Express and the Star onto the tour, at a cost of £10,000 each. This, perhaps, was Napier-Bell's biggest mistake, for the mid-1980s tabloid wars were raging hard and no paper would allow the truth to get in the way of an eye-catching headline. To invite four writers, none of whom were rock-orientated, into the heart of a pop tour and expose them to all the little dramas and pockets of hedonism – even among the spliff-toking roadies – was surely asking for trouble. However, Napier-Bell reasoned the whole point was to push Wham! directly into the headlines. A dangerous policy indeed.

At the start of the trip the lads were photographed skipping jauntily through Heathrow, quite carried away by a spirit of adventure, but their mood had darkened considerably by the time they had reached the Regal Meridian Hotel in Hong Kong. They had had to barge through an unwelcoming local press pack, all of whom fired barbed questions at them about the apparently inflated ticket prices for the Hong Kong shows. (The brief visit to Hong Kong was intended as both a warm-up for China and a method of clawing back some of the costs of the trip. Ticket prices were admittedly on the heavy side. In Hong Kong they were £22. In China, the cost of admission was £1.45.)

This little spat was followed by the news that all four British tabloids had – surprise, surprise – broken their promise to catch up with the tour in China and had arrived in Hong Kong, hungry for 'warm-up' stories. At this point, Napier-Bell's judgement was, perhaps, somewhat suspect.

Michael

There was a small incident when George Michael, naturally desperate for some pre-gig space, felt the need to distance himself from the suffocating, obsessive media circus, and forcibly ejected Anderson's omnipresent camera crew from his room. It was the moment when the star simply had to say: 'Enough!'

Alas, the baying hacks were never going to allow this opportunity to slip by and the Mirror's hugely successful John Blake, the man who had virtually instigated the tabloid's feverish intrusion into the world of pop, immediately wired back a story with the headline: 'Wham! Star Cracks Up and Cries'. The story told a sorry if rather laboured tale of how a nice, smiley, jaunty chap from Bushey had been transformed into an introverted, moody depressive. The fabrication was, of course, outrageous but, frankly, par for the course during this spell of tabloid war. The story, with added musings and quotes, rippled out messily through the nationals before coming to rest on the front pages of just about every regional daily newspaper in Britain. (One example was on the rain-lashed pavements of Manchester, where the Evening News boards suggested that Wham! had been involved in some kind of serious international incident. And all because George Michael had wanted half an hour's rest.)

Although Napier-Bell castigated Blake for unleashing this story, the writer would later defend his position thus, as delivered to writer Johnny Rogan: 'That was when things [between the warring tabloids] got really heavy. It was out-and-out war. George Michael actually did throw a wobbler, and there was a bit of a fracas. Everybody was a little hysterical. That particular trip was the worst pop trip I've ever been on in my life. Wham! had been on holiday having

finished their hard work and then Simon set up all these concerts. It was like being called back from school holidays and told to go to China. They hated it, so consequently they were very hostile and unpleasant, and the whole trip wasn't much fun.'

That night, a sweat-soaked George Michael bounced triumphantly off the stage at the end of the set at Hong Kong's Coliseum and squared up to the snapping press pack with the words: 'Do I look like I'm cracking up?' This remark proved cleverer than he could possibly have imagined for the Daily Mail, not officially on the trip, decided to take the opposite tack and furiously defended the star, all but accusing Blake of creating a complete and dangerous fabrication. But things were stranger still in China. Much stranger. Wham! had been fed reports of mile-long queues for tickets, of near hysteria, of a physical authoritarian presence. The queue stories were true – odd, as no one in China had actually heard of Wham! – but the hysteria was another press fabrication. The entourage was somewhat surprised to find that no fans were assembled to greet them at Peking Airport and they were transferred quietly to their hotel, trying hard not to be fazed by the sense of anticlimax.

More pleasing, perhaps, was the realisation that Peking didn't resemble a sombre, greying communist city but that on the streets, in the shops, in the hotels, there were plentiful signs of encroaching westernisation. Nevertheless, few people on this tour were in any doubt that every move the band made, whether onstage or during their many PR gatherings, would be painfully scrutinised by the paranoid 'hard left'. Every example of western culture, whether the arrival of Wham! or of Levis, would cause ripples of unease

to permeate through the rigid political system. Nor was anyone in any doubt that this was more, much more, than a mere exercise in entertainment. The Wham! boys, however, were probably the perfect ambassadors for western pop. There were no signs of subversion showing through their clean-cut image, which had already been massively overstated in the Chinese press, and the boys, warming to their role, behaved impeccably. Famously, they sauntered along the Great Wall of China with Napier-Bell, and the resulting press shots provided him, at last, with some kind of return for his immense investment. George Michael even delivered an eloquent speech to a curious assembly at the Chinese Youth Federation Banquet. Against the odds, things were suddenly looking good. Tapes of Make It Big - many of them, much to Napier-

Bell's consternation, sold through the 'unofficial' black market, and some clumsily pirated - had educated the fans in the music of Wham!. This proved both heartbreaking and welcoming for the band. As they watched their chance of swift commercial profits vanish as the hidden forces of a corrupt system seized control, they could only reflect that, to the average Chinese youth, Wham! was western pop music. In this strange, enormous country, they were instant megastars.

The first gig took place in the Workers Gymnasium on Sunday 7 April 1985. Ten thousand fans, having survived a body-popping support act called Trevor - their first view of western pop - greeted Wham! in an eerily reserved, respectful manner. Unaware that a tannoy announcement had warned the audience that 'dancing is not allowed' during Trevor's peculiar act, the Wham! boys wandered into the spotlight to the restrained opening chords of Wake Me Up Before You Go Go, and the absurd (in this context) opening chant of 'Jitterbug'.

Staring out into the crowd, George saw not the swaying hysterical mass that had been the norm, but an amorphous blob of mature blue-clad Chinese, all leaning forward in their chairs to study this strange new western phenomenon. As if the audience were not low-key enough, the first three rows comprised unsmiling members of officialdom. It was arguably the most surreal start to any concert in pop history. Wham! pushed their way into the set, with George hurtling across the stage, engaging in rhythmic gyrations that would shame a young Elvis Presley, and just dancing his heart out in front of three rows of stern faces. Pepsi and Shirlie must also have felt terrifyingly vulnerable as they strode to the front of the stage, glamorously attired in short leather skirts. A ripple of enthusiasm, but only a ripple, greeted Careless Whisper – Wham! owed even this small display of recognition to Napier-Bell who had so cleverly arranged for various bizarre and inept Hong Kong artists to record the song six months previously. Matters improved during the second half of the show and, much to George's delight and relief, a small number of apparently 'tuned-in' Wham! devotees started to dance and wave their programmes in the air during Freedom. This, needless to say, was treated like an act of mass rebellion, and the security officers began to hover menacingly over the dancers, forcing them to cease this dangerous juvenile nonsense and sit down. One youth was forcibly ejected for smoking a cigarette, while another was grasped from behind and pulled into the aisle. His crime? To clap his hands in the air.

The concert ended abruptly with precision timing and Wham!, more bewildered than hurt, strode from the stage to a trickle of faint and no doubt courageous applause. No encore, of course, was allowed or delivered yet as the band slumped into an anticlimactic huddle backstage, shrugging and casting questioning glances at each other, the crowd were wandering out onto the streets of Peking, the smiles on their faces betraying their subversive secret. They had actually enjoyed themselves. Officialdom, however, refused to smile and, although Xiao Hua, the ageing vice-chairman of the Chinese People's Consultative Conference feigned enjoyment, many of his surrounding aids stayed resolutely grim-faced at a performance that was inappropriate for China. Despite all that, it was still regarded as a success. Nobody expected anything remotely resembling a western concert. Later, George would reflect on the event: 'There is a huge cultural difference, which there is no way you are going to cross in an hour and a half. I turned my microphone down. I didn't do anything particularly sexy, which is not my usual angle. We noticed the police were very nervous about the possibility of everyone joining in. But I wonder what they could have expected. They knew we were a dance band.'

Meanwhile, with Napier-Bell fiddling more and more nervously with his pocket calculator, the Lindsay Anderson film was becoming increasingly problematic. Anderson complained that neither George nor Andrew had shown the slightest interest in the film, refusing, on a number of occasions, to talk to the camera and being, in Anderson's words, 'generally conceited'. Anderson's unease was intensified by the fact that – unbelievable as it may seem – he had

fallen from the Great Wall and although no serious damage had been done, he was wheelchair-bound and irritable for the remainder of the trip.

With the entourage steadying itself for the Canton lap of the journey, and with a few hacks jumping ship and heading back to London, it seemed that things couldn't really get any worse. But they did. Immediately. Horribly. With the tour party on board Flight CAA 1301 bound for Canton, events tripped into the farcical. Towards the back of the plane, Pepsi and Shirlie were slumped wearily next to the band's Portuguese trumpet player, Raul De Oliviera. Both girls would, in retrospect, comment that Raul seemed to be suffering a disproportionate amount of stress during the tour. No one, however, could have predicted the extent of his breakdown. Suddenly, as the plane went into a little turbulence, Raul, who had been muttering incoherently throughout the take-off, fell into a fit in his seat, holding his stomach and screaming uncontrollably. As Pepsi and Shirlie cowered in the adjoining seats, Raul grasped a pen knife and appeared to stab himself in the stomach. Through a barrage of general passenger panic and Raul's increasingly deafening screams, two security men managed, finally, to overpower him – although his demonic sobbing still unsettled the nearby passengers.

At this point, with the tension high, the plane plunged unexpectedly downwards, throwing the passengers into a scene of nightmarish horror. Ten minutes later, with the plane safely back on the Peking tarmac, Raul was duly led away. From the plane, all that could be heard were the muffled squeals of a distorted trumpet as Raul attempted, most disturbingly, to perform The Legion's Last Patrol. A deathly silence fell over the passengers – most, if not all, of whom now firmly wished to return swiftly to Britain. The last gig in Canton would surely be overshadowed by a feeling of doom?

The incident which, admittedly, could have been very nasty indeed, sent the tabloids into a frenzied scramble to produce the most eye-catching headlines. 'Wham! Man in Hari Kiri Terror' screamed The Sun, cloaking its lead paragraph in enough ambiguity to cause feverish George Michael fans to hand their money over only to discover that their hero hadn't, actually, been involved at all. Even the Daily Telegraph allowed its boards across the country to bellow the misleading, but undeniably true 'Wham! Man Goes Berserk!' headline. The headline writers were locked in combat and in the ensuing scramble, most of the genuine facts were hopelessly lost. Only one thing was certain. The tour of China had been expensive, traumatic and filled with a sense of foreboding.

In an astonishing interview with Smash Hits, Shirlie Holliman defied the Nomis team and unleashed a stream of frustration into the astonished reporter's tape machine. 'I think what we are doing here is bad. I don't want to sound funny or anything, but I don't think it's right that we are playing here. People here are sad, they want freedom but are not allowed to have it and, in a way, we are giving them a taste of something they can't really have. I just think it was awful how that boy was taken out of last night's concert and beaten. If we hadn't come here, that wouldn't have happened. I just want to go home.'

But despite all this and against all the odds,

the date at the Zhongshan Stadium in Canton proved to be mercifully free of the stringent official scrutiny of Peking. Canton's close proximity to Hong Kong ensured a certain liberalism. Most of the security guards, as well as the crowd, seemed curiously well versed in Wham! numbers and George Michael, astonished and delighted to be standing in front of a comparatively responsive audience, turned up the heat and dropped the nervy constraints he had sensibly imposed on himself in Peking. A sense of relief flooded the stage and the previously terrified Pepsi and Shirlie allowed themselves to relax once more, genuine smiles replacing the plastic grins of Peking.

The Canton show preceded a couple of days' rest for the band, who were still clearly irritated by the omnipresent film camera: 'I can't turn off. I just can't turn off. What do you want? Do you expect me to perform twenty-four hours a day?' complained George Michael to the conciliatory Jazz Summers. 'Just go with it. Forget the cameras, that's the whole idea. Be natural,' he replied, although he surely knew the impossibility of such advice.

But despite such distractions, Wham! spent their time in tourist mode, drifting aimlessly through Canton, even stopping off at the odd rather dubious-looking bar. Before long, however, the sheer hot, sticky, nauseatingly aromatic sensations of Canton's endless downbeat market areas began to take their toll on the Wham! entourage, and their touristic glee was, indeed, brief. Canton, unlike Hong Kong, Singapore or even Peking, prefers not to disguise its poverty; nor, for that matter, does it attempt to soften the nature of its butchery. Before long, sickened by the sight of unidentifiable skinned animals swinging from numerous hooks, the band returned to the comforts of their five-star hotel and drank their way through a particularly raucous evening. To some, this may have seemed like an example of typically shallow rock'n'roll excess. It wasn't. Wham!, for the first time in their lives, had met genuine poverty head on. Their hedonism, that evening, was simply an immediate escape – from both Canton and frankly, from Wham!. From everything.

They say the best way to blast through the horrors of a hangover is to indulge in overt physical activity, and the next day was highlighted by a musicians versus roadcrew soccer match, a frantic affair during which George and Andrew reverted to Bushey-schoolboy mode. It was another escape and, for a while, the duo lost themselves in nostalgia. It was short-lived, of course, for within hours they were bumbling through brief speeches at another banquet designed to ease open commercial channels that barely existed.

Once again that night George, Andrew, Pepsi and Shirlie fell into a cushioning alcoholic haze. And, before they had risen bleary-eyed and disorientated the next day, Simon Napier-Bell and Jazz Summers had orchestrated a press conference during which plans for rushing through a tape of Wham! recordings – containing selections from Fantastic and Make It Big – were unleashed onto the unstable Chinese market. Weirdly, this was swiftly followed by a further compilation containing a mixture of Wham! original recordings and cover versions of Wham! songs performed by ChengFang Yeun, China's foremost pop singer.

Weird indeed but even weirder still was the fact that, despite her undoubted fame, China's leading chanteuse was allowed to receive only the standard £15 per week wage. Wham! immediately smashed this piece of communist nonsense by offering her 1 per cent of the total income from the recordings. A mere gesture or a breakthrough for capitalism? Probably the latter and George Michael promised, earnestly, that he would make sure the payments actually got through to her. They were small things – that gesture, the tour: fine for the Wham! commercial machine and for the publicity but beyond that, very small indeed.

Back in London at a meeting with his favourite journalist Tony Parsons from The Face, George wasted no time in stating his feelings with regard to the entire fiasco: 'The basic reason for going to China was to introduce our wonderful culture. It was to do something. Just for once it was nice that you were the first and, quite possibly, the last. There is a certain privilege attached to that.

'But once we got there I just thought the whole thing was a shambles. What was basically going on was that the Chinese government was trying to encourage the western world to accept Chinese product. They were saying, "Look, we have our arms open, we are going to accept western music." That was total bollocks. They used us. We were a propaganda item.'

If nothing else, George's outburst, coupled with a similar sneer from Andrew Ridgeley in Smash Hits, served to answer the frequent criticisms that Wham! had evolved into Nomis puppets. If this were so – and it so clearly wasn't, for Nomis were terrified of George's mood swings – then the management team had certainly failed to cap the natural 'loose cannon' antics of both Wham! stars.

Michael

Few people would deny that the dynamics of Wham! had grown increasingly twisted. George had always held the power, of course, but the glamour and verve of Andrew and to a lesser extent the two girls had always seemed essential, too. They broadened the appeal and the visuals.

But the portents of Careless Whisper couldn't be ignored for much longer. To the delight of the mischievous tabloids, the talent and potential of George was beginning to weigh too heavily on the structure of a band designed only as a vehicle for lightweight pop. This imbalance seemed more and more obvious as time passed.

The split, which had always loomed on the horizon, edged a little closer in May 1985 when George Michael was invited by Stevie Wonder, no less, to perform at the hugely prestigious Motown Returns to the Apollo event. A number of influential US music-business heads began to turn as Michael slotted in with alarming ease next to Wonder and Smokey Robinson. Even the unflappable George must have been a little fazed when Robinson crooned his way through a top-bracket cabaret version of Careless Whisper.

A small picture in a Rolling Stone news item perfectly captured the moment. As Smokey Robinson chats into the mic in the foreground, behind him, grainy and melting into the shadows, can be seen the face of George Michael. A face exuding pride. This could have been the moment when George realised that he really had, in the true international sense of the phrase, 'made it big'. It could also have been the moment when it became clear that Wham! would not be able to hold him much longer.

Back in Britain, however, the revolution instigated by Geldof, Midge Ure and the Band Aid

Michael

phenomenon was exploding into something even bigger, something that would, literally, capture the imagination of the entire western world. On 13 July 1985, the Live Aid events at Wembley and Philadelphia altered for ever people's perception of pop and rock music. Everything changed. Before the bleary television eyes of millions, an unlikely bond was forged between the famine-ravaged reality of Ethiopia and the gushing sycophancy of the rock and pop business. How ironic, one might have thought, to note that the pivotal charity event of the century should have been inspired by the most shameless paparazzi posers of London's pop elite – Bob and Paula, as Hampstead-ised as an antique pine

table. These people even called their first daughter Fifi Trixibelle!

And yet nobody ever doubted that Live Aid was instigated with the best of intentions. Nobody doubted, either, that every artist who performed was wholly devoted to the cause. That stated, the gathering of so many egos in one stadium on one day proved endlessly fascinating. It was also – and the record companies knew this – a quite fantastic marketing exercise. Especially for the pop acts of the day best suited to stadium performance. In twenty minutes, for example, U2's majestic, anthemic performance saw them evolve into a top-flight international-stadium rock act. Queen's pulsating, parodic splendour seemed to gain extra power and Freddie Mercury, previously derided by the critics for his hackneyed posturing, was forgiven, loved even, by the very same people after Live Aid. As stated, the event had the power to alter people's perceptions. Things changed.

They certainly changed for Wham!. One might have expected them to explode onstage and burst into a frantic live megamix of greatest hits, bouncing around with youthful glee, and providing a welcome antithesis to ageing rockers like the Who and Status Quo, who opened the show. But the Wham! set was used to display the rapidly maturing talents of George Michael. Indeed, George was introduced by his Watford buddy Elton John, and their version of Don't Let The Sun Go Down On Me – with George's rich voice backed by Elton John's piano – seemed to instantly expand George's prestige. One could have been forgiven for failing to notice the superfluous backing vocals of Kiki Dee and Andrew Ridgeley.

But it was probably Jazz Summers who gazed upon Wham!'s contribution to Live Aid with the greatest degree of satisfaction. While drifting along with Napier-Bell's Chinese dream, Summers had been devoting his time, again cleverly, to America, nurturing new contacts, tapping precociously on the office doors of high-powered executives and generally examining the complex, extraordinary and endlessly fascinating network that controlled the American music business. This network had been jolted in recent years by the arrival of the twenty-four-hour musical television station MTV.

MTV had proven perfect for Wham!, whose lush, yuppified videos settled neatly into place, upsetting nobody while powering three Wham! singles to the No 1 spot – a quite extraordinary achievement considering the continuing failure of so many promising British acts to capture the imagination of America's surprisingly conservative youth. But Summers knew that to make a lasting impression in America and to attain Stateside longevity, it was essential to perform regularly on the stadium circuit. His ambitions at this level preceded Live Aid by twelve months. During that time he had deflected the pompous American promoters who, ignoring the revolution of MTV, repeatedly informed him that Wham! would have to climb the live-act ladder slowly, endlessly working the extensive US club circuit. Undoubtedly George Michael's side-by-side appearance with Elton John at Live Aid helped blast through such barriers.

Elton John's name carried enormous weight with American promoters. Summers knew this and wasn't surprised to find his telephone constantly bursting into life, to be followed by the excitable voice of a previously lukewarm US promoter. He knew Wham! could do it, but one thing worried him.

'George Michael was still weary of touring,' he said, 'and simply wasn't thrilled by the prospect of taking the whole entourage to America. I told him that, for the sake of his future, whether it be with Wham! or not, he simply had to perform in front of as many people as possible. He wasn't convinced but I knew, secretly, he didn't want to be just another MTV video band. What's more, Andrew wasn't too happy about it, Simon wasn't convinced and Morrison/Leahy were strangely uncertain.

'I remember we had a Wham! summit meeting about it and I lost the vote. It would have been easy for me to go with the flow, but I have never

'I'm sick of people treating me like I've only got one brain cell and only three lines of conversation'

George Michael

believed in doing things the easy way. I knew my way would be difficult for the band but I knew, also, that it was the only way to create something that would be really important and lasting. And George, I knew, would benefit the most.'

Summers' argument fell on deaf ears. Not surprising, since the China escapade had kicked the enthusiasm out of everyone concerned. Summers knew that only a miracle would rescue his plans. Incredibly, within a week of that meeting, the miracle happened. Over in Miami, a radio station had mistakenly been fed information that Wham! would be performing a local concert on 31 May. The date had not been confirmed, but during the course of one weekend, 30,000 tickets were sold without any advertising at all. This stunning response was all the ammunition Summers needed. The Nomis team agreed and George and Andrew, their egos

well and truly bolstered by this bizarre twist, found all their pre-China enthusiasm returning. Summers excitedly picked up the phone. The Wham! tour of America would proceed, and quickly.

It wasn't by any means an extensive tour. Just eight shows in America and one in Canada, playing to average crowds of more than 40,000. George, keen to display an image rather more mature than the sun-tanned, streaky-haired holiday boy of the Wham! videos, arrived in the States with a sexier, older, darker look, complete with leather gloves and an impossible ever-present five-o'-clock shadow gracing his cheeks.

In contrast to China, the tour proved a commercial success (despite the odd scurrilous 'Wham! Flop in States' headline back in Britain), although it was not without incident. The only downside for George was his inability to sink into the overwhelmingly gushing horror of the US record biz, an unholy conveyor belt of grinning, hand-pumping, back-slapping jokers. Although Summers had attempted to control George Michael's exposure to this disturbing phenomenon – he was terrified of unduly upsetting his star – he knew that to progress, George would have to play it the American way. But it was something that didn't sit well with him at all. It still doesn't. His natural revulsion when faced with sycophants would eventually seep into his songwriting (listen to Star People on Older).

The tour was dented slightly by an incident in Miami, while the band were relaxing post-gig in a suitably laid-back local nightclub. Wham!'s dreadlocked bassist, Deon Estes, had been chatting amiably to a girl at the bar when, for reasons that never came to light, she pulled a revolver from her handbag and began waving it around the room, at one point aiming it directly at the Wham! entourage. Only the skillful intervention of a particularly alert Wham! minder managed to prevent the incident from turning nasty. After Miami, needless to say, George and Andrew felt it necessary to hide behind a larger buffer of security.

In the States, Wham! had remained sensibly aloof from the vultures that populated the music press. This didn't sit well with the critics, who did not lavish the band with dizzying praise but, unlike the music press in Britain, they were not offended by the sight of rampant pop commercialism, either. Back in England, relationships with the media reached crisis point on two levels.

The tabloids seemed to have sharpened their knives and rather cruelly exaggerated Andrew Ridgeley's jet-setting, nightclubbing, girl-grabbing antics, turning his public image into sheer caricature. It didn't help that his tempestuous relationship with Shirlie Holliman had finally fizzled out and as if to heighten the split, the press immediately picked up on her rather swift engagement to the Spandau Ballet bass player and actor Martin Kemp. Not that Andrew was particularly slow to seek alternative female companionship, for soon the tabloid papers were filled with snapshots featuring him with Donia Fiorentine, the beautiful ex-teenage fiancee of Miami Vice star Don Johnson. It could have been suggested that Donia only went for men who wore terrible armless pastel-coloured jackets.

Indeed, Andrew's image was, in contrast to the darkening looks of George, still distinctly pastel-coloured, sockless and shamelessly archetypal of the 1980s. His spate of bad PR was completed by a series of motor-racing accidents, which excited further ridicule in the tabloids. Poor Andrew, it seemed, just couldn't do anything right.

With the paparazzi spotlight firmly fixed on the hapless Andrew, George ducked firmly out of sight, rarely surfacing from his fashionable Knightsbridge flat, writing songs and, more often than not, refusing to answer the phone. Jazz Summers, in particular, was beginning to worry about his star's state of isolation.

'It was a worry because I knew that George wasn't particularly happy. He was clearly moving from being a pop star to an artist of significance. There was no doubt about that, and yet he hadn't captured the attention of any of the more serious music critics. China had changed Wham!'s commercial status but not their critical status.'

It was simple. George was longing to be hip.

And not since Dave McCullouch's early writings on Wham! had he been afforded that honour. In truth, he was still secretly smarting from the Morley drubbing and, devouring the music press each week, he loathed the way in which Wham! were still regarded as a teen gimmick, to be overlooked in favour of a barrage of grey-clad, tuneless oiks from Birmingham and Manchester who existed only to emulate their precious hero, Morrissey.

Summers understood that, in Britain at least, if Wham! were to become a more lasting fixture, it was essential for them to encourage the seeds of serious critical consideration in the pages of the inky weeklies. As it turned out, a Summers-instigated article, written by Danny Kelly, would do little to quell George's unease. Nevertheless, his anger was allowed to spill into print.

'I need something where I'm written about intelligently, even if it's a slag-off. I'm sick of people treating me like I've only got one brain cell and only three lines of conversation. I'm sick of being presented in one-line quotes, and I'm sick of walking into rooms full of strangers who have a totally wrong idea about me.'

An odd line indeed. Was this George Michael attempting, as writer Johnny Rogan noted, to state that he was 'sick' of Wham!? Certainly his recent unease with the superficial excess in America, which had made him feel very much like lightweight product, lurked in the undertone of his phrases. Further hints that George was finally looking beyond Wham! were to be found in his laughter as Kelly reeled off a list of Andrew's nightclubbing exploits. Again the article was less than kind to Andrew, condemning him as 'a mobile vomit fountain', which must have surely hurt. The article wasn't granted as much space in

the NME as Summers would have liked, or George deserved. Perhaps this was because George refused to be drawn on Kelly's strange attempts to capture a 'gay exclusive' angle, although he did seem happy to remain ambiguous on that point.

Another irony clouded this attempt to 'deepen' George's image. It coincided with the release of what was arguably Wham!'s lightest single, the tumbling, effervescent I'm Your Man, which George had dashed off during an internal flight on the American tour. A sure-fire No 1, without doubt, but a song that barely hinted at the writing maturity inherent in both the tracks George had been working on at home, or the sublime, captivating funk that made it onto the flip side of Last Christmas, entitled Everything She Wants – or, for that matter, The Edge Of Heaven, so effectively previewed during the American tour.

At this point in George's career, one might have expected to see a different side of Wham!. On the other hand, the schizophrenia of his songwriting seemed blatantly obvious to Nomis who, just as I'm Your Man took the old-fashioned image of Wham! back to the top of the charts, were presented with a demo of the captivating, fascinatingly introspective A Different Corner (destined to become George Michael's oddest No1 single).

Says Summers: 'Yes, it was obvious that George was writing songs on two separate levels and it also occurred to us that he was finding this increasingly difficult. I'm Your Man was released partly because he was saving the deeper stuff for his solo career. That was what was occupying his mind at the time.'

Michael

George

9 the final

Shortly before Christmas 1985, George Michael and Andrew Ridgeley came to the inevitable conclusion that Wham! would split during the course of the following year. The Press had, for some time, hinted that George was being kind to Andrew by keeping the act together. It was generally held that George would be the first former teen-scream idol to cross-over to an adult audience when he finally left Wham!. Even Andrew had to admit that Wham! had been shackling the natural course of George's songwriting. He had been in no doubt, ever since his partner had released the sublime Careless Whisper, of the inevitability of the split, and seemed well prepared.

One thing still united the pair, however. They were determined to bow out in an unprecedented manner. No way would Wham! be allowed to settle into pop history with a string of minor hit records to their name. They would have to go out with a bang. With a gigantic concert and, perhaps, a massive, climactic album. Only on this point was George resistant. In his mind he was already firmly entrenched in his solo career. Nobody at Nomis was at all surprised by the decision. Napier-Bell had always maintained that Wham! would last two, maybe three years at most. And at Nomis, the wind of change was most definitely in the air. Nomis itself was about to be sold to a public company.

This curious shift had started when Summers and Napier-Bell had lunched with promoter Harvey Goldsmith back in 1984. Goldsmith informed them that, following a series of lofty deals, he was now playing for very high stakes. His company, Goldsmith Entertainments, had merged with another, Hotel Television Network Ltd, to form Allied Entertainments. In turn, this

66

Saturday 28 June 1986 – Wembley Stadium

Michael

'This must be the only business in the world where you can have so much money and no one to answer to'

George Michael

had been swallowed up by the mighty Kunick Leisure, owners of the London Dungeon. Goldsmith stated that, if the opportunity came along, he would be most interested in acquiring Nomis, thereby allowing Summers and Napier-Bell the financial clout to be able to leap several steps up the managerial ladder. Dizzied, perhaps, by the complex network of Kunick companies, Napier-Bell and Summers had spent a good deal of 1985 pursuing this possibility, until eventually they met with Kunick Chairman David Hull. This meeting was firmly shunted into music-business legend by writer Johnny Rogan who reported in Wham! The Death Of A Supergroup the Nomis pair's incredulity when confronted by the question, 'Does the South African connection bother you?'

Despite being presented with all the Kunick facts, and despite poring endlessly over chunky Kunick folders, neither Summers nor Napier-Bell had noticed that a major Kunick shareholder, Sol Kerzner, was the owner of Sun Hotels International, a subsidiary of a large South African corporation. The connection with South Africa was, therefore, glaringly obvious and, at a time when the rock élite had rallied strongly against performing in Sun City, the move was liable to be followed by a mass of damning and, for Wham!, potentially damaging press reports. As it happened, neither Napier-Bell nor Jazz Summers was at all happy about the South African connection but, after giving it serious consideration, they decided that their part in the organisation would not be affected by it.

Subsequently, the deal, approaching a £5m investment in Nomis by Kunick, began to take its course. By March 1986, at Kunick's annual general meeting, the deal would be complete.

Back in November 1995, upon hearing of the proposed deal, George Michael had actually asked Napier-Bell about the South African connection and the manager pleaded absolute ignorance. To this day it seems difficult to believe that Summers and Napier-Bell didn't realise that Michael would object so strongly to this connection. It also seems odd that Kunick, who were so obviously expecting Wham! to be a major part of this deal, were unaware that the duo had already decided to split.

The situation duly exploded following the intervention of George Michael. He warned Nomis that either they pull out of the Kunick deal or Wham! would seek alternative management. Thus George was wholly absolved of any South African connection, leaving Nomis red-faced and staring at a vanishing figure of £5m as Kunick firmly withdrew their offer. All this happened in a few days. With Andrew Ridgeley ensconced somewhere in Monte Carlo and seemingly unaware of the situation, Nomis had allowed the celebrated 'biggest band in the world' to slip out of their grasp. A number of questions remained, and still remain, unanswered. How could Nomis not have seen the South African connection? How could they have entered into the deal knowing that Wham! were effectively splitting up? How could Kunick enter the deal without knowing that very same fact – especially after the spate of rumours in the press? How could Nomis not have anticipated George Michael's reaction? A curious bundle of questions, leaving just one thing certain: Wham! would split slap-bang in the middle of 1986.

The initial idea of the band going out on a triumphant concert and album changed slightly as George decided to angle his muse firmly

towards his impending solo career. Unwilling and, perhaps, unable to put his songwriting talents into reverse, he decided that his best new material might be wasted on a full Wham! album, and the proposed release was swiftly truncated into an EP. Before that, however, as if to cement his future course, came the prophetically entitled solo single A Different Corner. This provided an immense and somewhat unexpected new twist to George's songwriting prowess. Here we discovered a melodic delicacy that was quite the antithesis of the solid and traditional verse-chorus-verse-chorus pop chant of I'm Your Man. This hardly sounded like the same artist at all.

Although the remarkably introspective lyrics would echo through his later releases, they seemed conspicuous at the time, especially as the single climbed up a particularly feeble-sounding chart. How lonely the record seemed up there, amid so many tepid offerings, the sound of a man wistfully harking back to carefree days of youth, when life seem so exquisitely uncomplicated. It was a sad record – and Michael would, in later life, regard it as his most painful release, as well as an exorcism of sorts, for he had been suppressing this introspection and unhappiness for some time, and the songs of Wham! were simply not capable of carrying such emotion. If Careless Whisper can be seen, like Last Christmas, as a mini-lyrical soap opera, then A Different Corner was less obvious, far more intense, far more personal.

This boldly introspective approach would, in time, become a trademark of George Michael's solo career but, in 1986, it seemed strange, to say the least. But strangeness couldn't prevent the song from climbing to No 1, and the song would soon find an unlikely resting place next to the

pop hits of Wham! in teenage bedrooms across the country. But it was more than simply offering a new dimension to the fans. A Different Corner, like Careless Whisper and, perhaps, Last Christmas, managed to seep into the daily listening of a far more reserved audience. Either George Michael was, in terms of marketing, exceptionally clever, or just lucky, or both. By allowing his solo career to wedge itself into the final year of Wham!, he was creating a seamless transition.

A Different Corner was clever in other ways, too. It was to become the first No 1 record in pop history to be written, arranged, produced, performed and sung by the same person. Imagine that. So much for the notion of George Michael as a pop puppet. Strangely, perhaps, George's split from Nomis failed to herald a new era of liberation for the star. Rather than feeling free from the chains of a strong management team, he now found himself more and more deeply immersed in the complexities of running his own career. Slowly, under the guidance of his ex-tour manager Jake Duncan, a small but committed team was set up to run his affairs – at least until the swift public demise of Wham!. It wasn't a perfect set-up – a small office, staffed by a small and disparate army, all pushing to gain Michael's approval. Ludicrously, he found himself more an office manager than a pop artist, but he still felt compelled to vet each prospective member of staff.

At times, his understandable concern about his own affairs bordered on obsession. He trusted nobody and that, frankly, made him feel extremely lonely. Not that this was allowed to encroach on his ever-hardening image. Delighted to be the subject of a Julie Burchill interview in

The Times, an elated Michael exclaimed: 'This must be the only business in the world where you can have so much money and no one to answer to. What better job can you have?'

It is possible to trace the beginnings of the elegant though rather savagely businesslike routine of George Michael from this moment – a routine that would to some seem alarmingly, pretentiously 'starry'. But a routine, nonetheless, that would be essential. The paradox of George Michael was glaringly obvious. Although professing to loathe the 'star system' and all the sycophantic hypocrisy that revolved around it, he still imposed a benevolent despotism on all who worked for him. As a direct result of that loathesome sycophancy, he became wholly detached, aloof from some of his closest friends.

Was there no escape from this new regime? Actually, yes. In time, George would use his wealth to serve, more effectively than any other star alive, his charitable bent – but that wouldn't become apparent for some time. Back in the mid- to late-1980s, George Michael was, to all intents and purposes, as horrendously precious as Prince.

Wham!'s final flourish, set for Saturday 28 June 1986 at Wembley Stadium, was preceded by the release of their final and anticlimactic EP, fronted by the Edge of Heaven and featuring Where Did Our Love Go, Battlestations, and a subdued remix called Wham! Rap '86, featuring Elton John. More interesting was the video, shot in the dank confines of a mock rock club, filled with students from Epsom College of Arts. The youths had all been paid £30 beer money to spend an evening leaping up and down, waving their arms about in pseudo-frantic adulation. The video made odd viewing, with the Wham! boys gleefully parodying a rock gig and fading from

the screen to be replaced by the single word, 'Goodbye'.

Saturday 28 June 1986 Wembley Stadium

A disparate horde, 72,000 in total, snaked towards the twin towers, seeped into the stadium and then settled, a little too tightly packed, on the famous rectangle. Once past the badge-covered screamers – perhaps about 30 per cent of the total assembly – who jostled noisily and tearfully at the front, no discernible style of dress unified the crowd at all. Young, by and large, and distinctly 'non-rock', they had drifted to London from a hundred parochial towns. Office teams from Mansfield, a pack of 'schoolies' from Stoke-on-Trent, trainee nurses from Chelmsford and scores of young dating couples, garage mechanics perhaps, clutching their rather more hyper girlfriends as close as possible. They could have been plucked, at random, from any nightspot in the country.

They were simply a cross-section of the nation's youth. Ordinary, excitable, not particularly well behaved, and not menacing, either. Wham! fans together for the very last time. And together they howled at the sight of the eternally parodic Gary Glitter, performing at Wembley for the first time since 1972. They bounced merrily to Nick Heyward, whose run of Haircut 100 and solo hits were recent enough to be lodged, just, in the minds of the majority of the crowd. It was extremely hot – so hot that the stewards believed they had been given licence to dowse the crowd, especially the T-shirted girls, with jets of often unwelcome water. This official stupidity soon spread into the crowd where, alas, oafish lads fell into yob mode, squirting cans of lager over everyone and anyone, transforming a mild, good-natured pop event into artless idiocy.

Following this came a screening of the film that would have been Wham! In China: A Cultural Revolution, now transformed into the less ambitious, post-Anderson video project produced by Martin Lewis and Jazz Summers and blandly retitled Foreign Skies. At 7.35pm, four hours after Glitter's 'amusing' appearance, audience impatience was skillfully transformed into fevered anticipation as the familiar strains of Everything She Wants drifted over the crowd.

And suddenly, a leather-clad, stubble-faced, shorn-haired George Michael appeared, dancing alone apart from two anonymous and routine black dancers. The crowd's glee had exploded and died before the three supporting members of Wham! fell happily into George's slipstream, with Andrew hamming it up supremely, passing his cloak to a giggling Pepsi and Shirlie, their figures hugged by spray-on leather dresses. Following the sprightly choreography of Club Tropicana, George took hold of the microphone and, at last, added a touch of personality, of warmth to the proceedings.

'This is obviously the most important gig we have ever played,' he stressed, ignoring the resulting cheers. 'We've got four years of thank yous to say this evening and I know we are going to enjoy saying them, so let's get started.' And from that moment, things warmed up. George had made eye contact with the first few adoring rows of the crowd and their subsequent squeaky responses filtered across the stadium, setting things up nicely for sixty minutes of solid, back-to-back Wham! highlights, all delivered with the expected stunning choreography. George's galloping athleticism controlled the camp posturing of Andrew and the girls who, via a

series of deft costume changes, fell into rather crass parody spanning the history of rock'n'roll, although not in chronological order.

One hour in, with the infectious dancing having permeated the ranks of the police officers – unprecedented, surely – the garish, burly figure of Ronald McDonald sauntered cheekily onstage, causing the initial bewilderment in the crowd to transform into cheery recognition as, sitting behind a white grand piano, he was suddenly, quite clearly, revealed as being Elton John. He was no stranger, of course, to the vast, heady climes of enormous stadiums but his curious costume was perhaps an attempt to disguise his middle-aged girth, all the more obvious as he shared the stage with at least four examples of rather svelte youth.

The Edge of Heaven had passed before George fully acknowledged Elton John's presence with a somewhat dour run-through of Candle In The Wind, George's vocals adding an eerie edge to Elton's classic. Later in the surprisingly long set, Elton John returned, his tasteless McDonald creation abandoned in favour of a pink drape jacket, his head capped by a pink Mohican wig. Would he ever give up trying to upstage Wham!?

Meanwhile, to complete the atmosphere of pop-star chumminess, Duran Duran's Simon Le Bon – who, like Andrew, had found his true spiritual home in the posey South of France resorts of Nice, Juan Les Pins and Antibes, and who had also become a symbol of the sockless 1980s – joined George on vocals. And the final image, to accompanying wails of absurd grief from the crowd, saw George and Andrew clasped together, dripping with tears and sweat, waving a last goodbye to their fans. The spotlight died, and so did Wham!.

George

10 ———— faith

For George Michael fans, the Wembley final seemed aptly named for, rather like the climax to a particularly intense football season, it was immediately followed by the deadening silence of anticlimax – offset, perhaps, by repeated bedroom plays of The Final, Wham!'s Greatest Hits, captured in 12-inch glory on a limited-edition gold disc. This was the ultimate collectors' item, the final milking.

For George, who was already two No 1 singles into a solo career, vanishing from sight for a while was the wisest and most obvious tactic. However, four years spent at the epicentre of a violent vortex of pop hype was not an easy thing to escape. For him, the silence was not only deafening, but it allowed his previously suppressed personal problems to bubble up to the surface. It sounds like such a cliché – the star swamped by blindly adoring fans, yet privately

crying out for help, but this was the situation in which George found himself during the summer of 1986. And as the distracting, violent anarchy of his Wham! career vanished virtually overnight, he was left feeling as though he had been cast painfully adrift.

To complete this feeling, incredible as it may seem, George Michael had suffered a stunning personal heartbreak just prior to Wham!'s finale. This 'rejection' still managed to surface in the press, and the fact that George would not name the person in question – other than stating: 'I was infatuated and rejected for the first time in my life and it hurt like hell' – merely fuelled the outrageous press speculation. Who was this person? Was it a girl? Was he talking, however ambiguously, about the end of Wham!? Probably not but, other than allowing this self-pitying streak to spill over into an interview for Time Out,

74

'I was infatuated and rejected for
the first time in my life
and it hurt like hell'

Michael

he remained silent and turned his attention to a new, loving companion, Kathy Jeung.

George spent the final five months of 1986 struggling to adjust to his new solo status, leaving England and its baying tabloids for America where, at last, he could find some space. A period of detached hedonism ensued, with George sinking further into the welcoming arms of heavy alcohol bingeing. Occasionally he would raise his head to exclaim, often via some hastily arranged phone interview with the English press that, 'I had it all, everything I wanted. It was a terrible situation to be in because you just don't know where to go from that point.'

George's unease with the kind of situation that most people spend their entire lives dreaming of was undoubtedly rooted in his shy teenage existence, when very few of the local girls even bothered to glance his way. Ironically, the career that had changed his sexual fortunes had also caused his one truly meaningful relationship to collapse. That was the George Michael conundrum, and a situation that has beleaguered stars of stage, screen and music since the beginning of Hollywood and rock'n'roll respectively. The problem now was that he could no longer escape his troubles by falling into a state of laddish bonhomie with Andrew Ridgeley. Perhaps his former partner's input into the Wham! machine had been greater, on the personal side, than anyone could have imagined? His new girlfriend, the make-up artist and model Kathy Jeung, seemed naturally antipathetic towards the famous and her total lack of awe certainly helped matters, although their relationship was often, literally, rather distant. While she stayed firmly in LA, George flitted, often rather pointlessly, around the world, still

openly finding relief in alcohol and, many reporters noted, looking less and less like the vibrant pop star who had, just months previously, seemed so in control.

In situations like this, the ironies tend to pile up. How odd, then, to find that George had bumped into Andrew Ridgeley in Los Angeles and forced his bewildered ex-partner to 'go out on a bender'. In a bizarre parallel to the post-party meeting between the two pre-Wham! schoolboys, George once again poured his heart out to a startled Andrew, who accepted his role in this catharsis with good grace. Although George's attack of depression – probably fired by the added pressures of his impending solo career – was far from over, Andrew's 'pull yourself together' speech did seem to show him the light. George began funnelling his complex personal problems into his writing. It was his only true method of escape and his depression would soon haunt his recordings.

To George's delight, a recording he had made in the summer finally came to fruition, bolstering his ego and his career. In the spring, he had received a call from Arista, enquiring if he would like to perform a duet with Aretha Franklin. That call was heaven-sent, and presented him with a clear, unexpected chance to immediately prove that, upon leaving Wham!, he had taken several leaps up rock's precarious, hierarchical ladder. Although intelligent enough to realise that the resultant single, I Knew You Were Waiting, would provide the ageing Queen of Soul with a much-needed stab at a new, younger audience, he was more than happy to bask in her unimpeachable credibility. The liaison worked beautifully for both artists, scaling both US and British charts in January 1987 (in Britain , with exquisite irony, it

George receives a platinum disc for the Faith LP

George with girlfriend Kathy Jeung...

...and onstage at the Nelson Mandela concert at Wembley stadium

prevented Pepsi and Shirlie from attaining the top spot with their debut single, Heartache).

Yet again, George had arrived almost without effort at his natural chart position and Aretha Franklin, unused to such dizzying heights since the late 1960s, was secretly grateful. Not for the first time, George could look to the heavens and wonder if someone up there really was looking after him. I Knew You Were Waiting introduced him as a serious artist to the kind of audience, especially in America, who would have previously scorned his Wham! outpourings. This unexpected success would serve to strangle his bout of self-pity, for George was forced to admit that he had been dealt, yet again, a rare and enviable slice of luck.

A hint at the future direction of George's solo career could be gleaned from his appearance in the audience at a Prince concert in London in the autumn of 1986. It had been well known for some time that George had been an ardent admirer of the Minneapolis imp and his distinctive brand of delicate sexy funk. At one time, George cited Prince's Kiss as his favourite song, and echoes of that precision-funk masterpiece would soon be discovered in many corners of George's solo repertoire. He was particularly drawn to the sexual ambiguity that seemed to flow from Prince's 'in song' persona, an effect apparently exaggerated by tweaking the speed of Prince's voice (note also the wonderful role-reversal atmosphere on Prince's extraordinary Kiss video).

With Prince in mind, George penned a risqué number rather numbingly entitled Johnny Sex. It was written before his appearance at the International Aids Day event at Wembley Arena in April 1987, and therefore most definitely was not

a juvenile reference to the message of that day – a day when Paula Yates introduced George with the words, 'Everyone wants to bonk this man but, if you do, you must use a condom!'

But Johnny Sex was a definite attempt to stir up a little sexual fuss although, as he had originally intended to give the song to his friend David Austin for his solo career, it seems he wasn't deliberately courting controversy for himself. That said, it seemed a strange choice for his first solo single, even given its altered title, I Want Your Sex, and slightly softened sexual message. For Britain was then awash with governmental Aids awareness campaigns and, in this climate, any song openly championing the cause of instant sexual gratification would surely encourage adverse comment. Which it did. Immediately, George's old friends the British tabloids merged to form a very stupid beast and swung into the attack, castigating George for his sexual audacity while simultaneously continuing their holy tradition of publishing Page Three photo shoots.

The press furore didn't carry too much weight, however, and this fascinating single easily transcended such pseudo-pious objections. The truth is that the song was both an honestly sexual and an emotional plea to the opposite sex from a man who had, by the very nature of his work, encountered sexual adventure on a grand scale. Curiously, though, I Want Your Sex was attacked by the very same po-faced BBC executives who had banned Frankie Goes to Hollywood's mildly risqué Relax – thus causing it to become a massive worldwide hit – and George's record, likewise, defied a daytime ban by climbing to No 3. George should really have accepted the BBC ban, which probably enhanced his career, with good grace. He didn't, however, and duly instructed that no more records should be sent to Broadcasting House.

But the BBC were far from alone in their outrage. In America, the normally liberal MTV re-edited the video three times before deeming it acceptable. This was, perhaps, slightly more understandable, for the promo, featuring George's girlfriend Kathy Jeung, saw George blindfolding her before running through a series of sexual power antics resembling the Mickey Rourke/Kim Basinger relationship in the tastefully steamy Nine And A Half Weeks. MTV's reticence aside, I Want Your Sex placed George at No 2 in the Billboard Chart, nicely whetting appetites for his first solo album, initially entitled Kissing A Fool.

Before this, however, the voice of George, albeit in disguised mode, could be heard on the Boogie Box High version of the Bee Gees' Jive Talkin', a disc featuring his cousin, Andros Georgiou, and, on guitar, Nick Heyward. It was an unlikely little departure and one that saw Michael giving a brief nod to his days spent gyrating to Saturday Night Fever rather than cramming his portly young form into a bin liner and spouting artless punk slogans. Whatever his reasons for helping out – fun, probably – George's Midas touch seemed to work. Jive Talkin', not a great record by any means, still reached No 7 in Britain. Prior to the release of his album, George moved out to the rock-star belt of Hertfordshire and splashed out £1.3m on a country mansion, complete with a £25,000 home gymnasium and solarium. The purchase was all too much for The Sun newspaper, who duly went overboard, suggesting that George had been squandering his millions by going on an international orgy of

property purchasing. (Actually, the following year some substance was added to this angle. His Hertfordshire mansion would soon be joined by a £1m Knightsbridge penthouse plus three overseas properties and, within two years, his own private jet.)

The mighty Faith, yet another single from the album, had started life when a friend half-heartedly suggested that the star should write a rock'n'roll pastiche. Just two days later, Michael presented him with the Faith demo and offered the humorously smug words, 'You mean, like this?' How could it have been so easy? For Faith was a beautifully open working of Bo Diddley's box-guitar riff pumping away between neatly crafted, if rather meaningless, lyrics. While nodding towards the Sun sessions of Elvis Presley, Faith would also use the aforementioned echo of Prince's Kiss, an effect that would be duly enhanced by the 'choppy' video technique.

The song was welded to George's new, slightly courageous image, that of a cleaned-up, dusted-down mock rocker plucked straight from Marlon Brando's Wild One and served up in consumer-friendly form, without the merest hint of rebellion. Nevertheless, the stubble-chinned and leather-jacketed approach, which in England encouraged comparisons with the highly irritating Shakin' Stevens, seemed good enough to dispense with any lingering notions of boyishness and yet still managed to keep his sexual appeal on the boil.

The Faith album was released – to instant adulation from the fans and mixed critical reviews – in November 1987, and showed immediate signs of becoming a landmark record. It was mature, mid-Atlantic pop, full of intensely personal lyricism and a universe away from the

George

clumsy collections that had been passed off as Wham! albums. Here at last was the cementing of a George Michael 'sound' , a little too low-key for those with eclectic tastes, perhaps, but as introspective as it is possible to get while jostling for a place at the very top of the marketplace (and George's scary task, with this album, was to move up alongside Michael Jackson and Bruce Springsteen).

It would take two or three plays to realise thaton top of Faith's elegant, subtle backing, George had been having a good deal of fun, for the album is peppered with obtuse lyrical references. One thinks of Hand To Mouth, a savage attack on the Maggie Thatcher-fronted push to establish the UK as a new American state. (Ironic, considering Faith's mid-Atlantic feel.) Dig deeper into that song, as Bruce Dessau did for his book, George Michael, The Making Of A Superstar, and you'll uncover a reference to a mass shooting that was written, rather eerily, two weeks before Michael Ryan's rampage through the streets of Hungerford.

But freak references like that aside – and George has never attracted the kind of fan who scrutinises every word of his lyrics – Faith was cleverly constructed to attract strong interest in America. Still, it was difficult to see this album failing. The first three tracks – Faith, the sublime Father Figure, and I Want Your Sex – contained more variety, more depth and, most importantly, more promise than all the Wham! albums put together. Nevertheless, George was only too well aware that Wham! had only managed one hit album in the States, and Faith would, for better or worse, be seen as his pivotal release.

It was make or break time. He needn't have worried, though: Faith would hit the US No1 spot twice and spawn six massive US singles, before finishing the year by being voted Best Album at the Grammy Awards. In England the album's release was heralded by an unashamed £100,000 bash at London's Savoy hotel – effectively, if expensively, keeping George firmly on the front page of the tabloids. This did little to dispel his growing, and not particularly attractive 'yuppie of pop' image, especially as the party attracted just about every entertainment figure in London, from Bob Geldof to – gasp – Anne Diamond.

The lavish nature of this bash – paid for by Epic – was further reflected by another of George's Elvis-style post-Faith spending sprees, during which he purchased a Rolls-Royce for his father, a BMW for his sister Melanie, and a Toyota for Kathy Jeung. The link with Thatcherite yuppiedom was further sealed by a report in Money Magazine, which published a heavily hyped league table of the two hundred richest people in Great Britain. It was noted that George still had £13m to go before overtaking his idol, David Bowie. 'I'll pass him soon,' he glibly stated, before wisely adding, 'but that's not why I'm doing this. I'm not a breadhead, honestly I'm not. But it's nice to be up here, I can't deny that.'

Climbing to such heights certainly had its drawbacks. If the George of the 'Wham! in China' era had been tour-weary and jaded, then he would have to prepare himself a little better for the worldwide Faith Tour, an awesome 150-date marathon beginning in the infamous 11,000-seater Budokan Theatre in Japan, an arena filled with ghosts of great past performances, from Dylan to the Rolling Stones. That date and the long, long tour, snaking its way around the globe, would throw him into a permanently detached state, and touring mode would turn him into a man now solely responsible for an entire on-the-road army. Nobody told him that it would be easy but, then again, it seemed to George that no one else he had spoken to had faced the enormity of such a task (other than Elton, who winced at the prospect before offering his occasional help).

Realising the extent of these impending pressures, George submitted to the inevitable and called in the high-powered Hollywood management team of Michael Lippman and Robert Kahane. Immediately, things changed, and although to this day he professes to loathe the trappings of top-deck pop stardom, it seemed there would now be no going back. His aforementioned mock-aloofness was merely a stepping stone to the real thing.

A screen was placed around George Michael. Contact with him, even for relatively close friends, would be all but impossible for the duration of the tour. He had moved into the top league, into the 'star bubble'.

Once the obligatory worries about the sexual content of his show had been dealt with, Japan proved a perfect opener for the tour, with the largely sedate audience clapping politely between songs. It was an absurd scenario and a flashback to the China sojourn caused George to fall into a fit of mid-show giggles. One British tabloid reported this as 'George Michael Breaks Down Onstage!'. By the time the tour reached Australia, he was suffering from throat and back problems. Both affected him greatly. Irritatingly, he was forced to give up his favourite form of on tour recreation – tennis, a habit he had picked up from Elton John.

More press absurdities followed. Then, edging into Europe, faced with a demand from a predatory press pack larger than the audience of a mid-sized rock band, George Michael relented, broke his way out of his bubble of silence and held a press conference in a converted aircraft hanger above the Ahoy Stadium in Rotterdam. More than 200 journalists attended, the British contingent acting as always like a herd of rampant soccer fans. 'What I'm not here to do,' stressed Michael, 'is to make a series of denials into speculations about my private life.'

'We'll just make it up anyway,' chirped one waggish Brit not blessed with the gift of tact. As it turned out, the British press were swamped by the gushing sycophancy of their European counterparts, who seemed to have all the critical faculties of a pack of fanzine writers. Eventually, the Mirror's Gill Pringle broke through the deadlock with a typically saucy enquiry about whether George had had an HIV test or not. His answer, a curt 'No', was seemingly enough to guarantee a huge splash the next morning, telling the story of how George Michael was so terrified of Aids that he had refused to face facts and have a test.

As the tour trundled on, George kept weariness at bay by remaining aloof from the ever-present circulating hangers-on, the press – a constantly changing beast – as well as from his musicians. This was not the good ship Camaraderie. It was tainted by stark, workman-like professionalism, making it lucrative but rather cool. Whether this coldness permeated the music was open to question. George's onstage efforts were usually enough to carry the sets to a triumphant conclusion. To be fair to George, he was quite correct in trying to prevent this enormous tour from snowballing into a hedonistic orgy, crashing from hotel bar to hotel

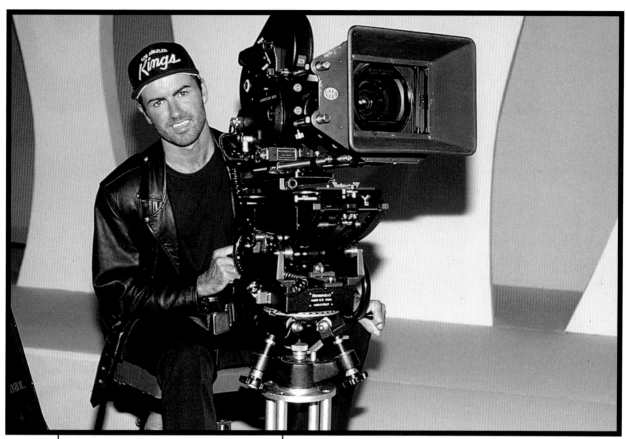

George on the set of Too Funky

'I'm not a breadhead, honestly I'm not. But it's nice to be up here, I can't deny that'

George Michael

bar and becoming increasingly loose and disjointed. The pressure was on him and despite a mid-tour problem with throat nodules – the result of a lack of voice training – he grimly carried on, promising himself that never again would he imprison himself within the confines of a worldwide tour.

Over in England, rumours about the nature of George's sexual preferences were stirred into life, again by The Sun who ran an outrageously scurrilous piece outing the – and these are their words, not mine-' Poofs of Pop'. This disgraceful post-Aids slur cited such artists as Boy George, David Bowie, Elton John and, gasp, the Village People. This example of supreme investigative journalism did not, of course, mention the name of George Michael. However, just as a teaser, the

on the set of Too Funky with Linda Evangelista...

and friends??!!

article was topped by his photograph. Clearly The Sun was playing games. George's response has not been recorded.

But this same paper welcomed George as the tour burst into Britain during June 1988. To the relief of the musicians, who were beginning to tire of his despotism, his demeanour seemed to improve drastically as he settled cosily into a five-night extravaganza at Earl's Court. The most important date, perhaps, took place on Saturday 11 June, when his gig in the capital took place on the same day as a huge event at Wembley Stadium to celebrate the seventieth birthday of the still-jailed African National Congress leader Nelson Mandela.

As the Wembley bash began, like Live Aid, at midday, George was delighted to pledge his support with an appearance. It would be refreshing for him, also, to break from the staid conformity of his Faith set and, wisely, he chose to run through some of his favourite tracks instead.

Bouncing onstage after Sting's opening splash, he excited the crowd with a stunning and unexpected rendition of Marvin Gaye's classic, Sexual Healing – a difficult song to cover, to say the least. As was his second and final choice, Stevie Wonder's Ghetto Land, a noticeable slice of social comment on a day that sagged a little into rather distasteful musicianly backslapping. Back at Earl's Court, Britain could view at last the new, mature George Michael set, freed from the constraints and the rounded visuals of Wham!. The Faith songs seemed to soak through the sexual gymnastics, replacing the sheer thrust and vigour of the old days with a subtle, more professional funk.

The twist was obvious. While the visuals had dipped slightly, the quality of the music had risen considerably. It was now possible to listen to a George Michael show. The final, all-important forty-six-date leg of the tour, a trek across America, beckoned loudly and George's voice, though sounding quite exquisitely 'black' at Earl's Court, was very precariously balanced. Would it, could it last? No amount of high-priced medical attention could quell his anxiety, and his anxiety, of course, would sound in the tones of his voice. He simply had to relax. Not so easy when the most important two months of your life lie before you, arduous and daunting.

And all the while he would hear the spiteful murmurings of an indignant set of musicians, quietly rebelling against the tour's autocratic atmosphere, filling their time with an endless barrage of anti-George jokes, like the bitter boss-baiting lunchtime banter of factory workers. George knew all about this and although hurt – for he genuinely knew no other way of completing such a tour – regarded it as an inevitable if unfortunate price to pay for sitting at the top of the pack. Never again could he be one of the lads.

His worries about the success of the tour were, however, unfounded. By the time the George Michael entourage had landed in the States, the Faith album had moved mountains. Latterly regarded as one of the most successfully promoted debut albums in pop history, it was enough to boost George up into that hallowed territory occupied by Michael Jackson. In Britain his post-Wham! career had predictably levelled, allowing Faith to mop up the massive newlyweds market, providing him with slowly ascending sales and, for a while, diminishing critical success. Meanwhile, in America it was all systems go.

L to R: Demi Moore, Rob Lowe, GM and Daphne Zuniga

Unlike Britain, the US market is not affected by prejudicial trends. It was a case of, 'Hey, here's a white boy singing soul, and a bit of pop as well! Great!'

Even George himself, his confidence now running sky-high, admitted to a Rolling Stone writer: 'I can hardly believe it. It has been such hard work and it was all meticulously planned, but the fact that everything we have done in the past year has succeeded absolutely, and has even gone beyond expectations, is simply amazing. Maybe I'm just suited to America.'

Ironic, of course, as Wham! were initially considered a profoundly British phenomenon. Rolling Stone magazine would neatly sum up his Stateside appeal by noting that 'George Michael exudes the kind of Britishness that Americans are complete suckers for, while the British themselves are not so sure.'

George

11 listen without prejudice

And following the breakthrough year, the anticlimax. Mercifully perhaps, things slowed for George Michael in 1989. From the safety of his new solid base of megastardom, he could now afford to relax, sit back and plan his next move – while naturally sweeping up no small number of prestigious music-industry awards: January – the sixteenth annual American Music Awards voted him Favourite Male Artist, as well as encumbering him with a stack of R&B awards. April – Faith won the International Hit of the Year Award. Also in April, George won Songwriter of the Year at the Ivor Novello Awards at London's Grosvenor House. June – George won the Silver Clef Award at the Nordoff-Robins benefit lunch in London. September – Madonna presented George with the Video Vanguard Award at the Universal Amphitheatre in Los Angeles. All year, it seemed, we were gazing at his smiling, bearded face as he stumbled through acceptance speeches and accepted the hearty back slaps from grinning musical dignitaries.

1989 also merited a slight hardening of attitude from George who had started the year portentously by successfully renegotiating his contract with CBS. In June, he collected a reputed £100,000 in damages from his old friends The Sun after a lengthy battle against an article depicting George gatecrashing an Andrew Lloyd-Webber party and becoming abusively drunk. Whether George objected to the allegations of drunkenness or his lack of taste in tagging onto a Lloyd-Webber bash has never been disclosed. In 1989, in between his awards appearances and encouraging surges of writing, George divided his time between London and Los Angeles, while tramping about Hampstead Heath, laying low and slowly, steadily sinking back into recording mode.

Meanwhile Andrew's recording career, absurdly

90

minuscule by comparison, spluttered to an abrupt halt. One recalls hearing a top music-business lawyer screaming down a telephone the words, 'But Andrew, the record company need to hear at least one song before offering a deal.' One realised how Andrew's name might carry a few sales, but when the record, a hard-rock dirge called Shake, finally did surface the British public chose to ignore it completely in a rare display of excellent taste. Andrew and George had grown into the complete antithesis of each other.

But not everything worked so smoothly for George. The run-up period to his second solo album, Listen Without Prejudice, seemed plagued by rumours and false starts. Six months before its

release, the press were informed that they could expect a double album. This intriguing prospect was lessened as the rumour would, in time, truncate to a single album filled with ballads, to be swiftly followed by blast of funky outtakes. How odd. How unlikely.

Were these advance stories merely products of the busy imagination of his PR office? Quite possibly, but the truth was that George had scrapped a number of recordings and had duly thrown the staff at CBS/Sony into something of a quandary. Eventually, in June, they were presented with Listen Without Prejudice and, despite the album's low-key feel, the company seemed highly satisfied. George, sensing his power, once again began renegotiating the financial conditions of his recording deal. Something was niggling away in his mind. Meanwhile, this proposed double album was sliced in half and eventually surfaced, confusingly – and the confusion lingers still – as Listen Without Prejudice, Volume One.

Preceding the album's release by just two weeks came the single Praying For Time, an unexpectedly understated ballad that slowly grabbed the lapels of the casual listeners and drew them slowly in. It was, indeed, fascinating to hear the initially dismissive radio DJs change their minds as the haunting quality of the song began to take hold.

'I didn't like that at first but it's really growing on me now,' was the general angle as the song's majesty slowly began to dwarf the chart songs that hovered around it. Praying For Time, written, produced and performed totally by George, pushed him into a new area of 'sophisto-pop'. Now, it seemed, he had reached a level of elegance that no one during the days of Wham! could possibly have predicted.

In America, the single would become something of an anthem for US military personnel leaving for active service in the Gulf War. George would state: 'The song was just my idea of trying to figure out why it's so hard for people to be good to each other.' In Britain the single lodged itself at No 6 – a mystery, really, as it bore all the hallmarks of a lasting No 1. Perhaps people were holding out for the album. For Praying For Time does have the feeling of being part of a larger whole. The fans were not to be disappointed. The majestic production of Praying For Time flowed bravely across the entire album. Track two, Freedom '90, seemed to confirm this

instantly, as well as representing George's widened scope, coming complete with curiously controlled gospel chant. In Freedom '90, George bravely attempted to convey the notion that he wished to move away from selling himself as a physical persona – a theme that would hover over him for the next six years.

To clash with the album's release, the television institution known to the world as The South Bank Show chose to feature George as the first subject of the new series. If George Michael had pined for credible acceptance in England, then here it was. From this point on, he could be assured that his music would grace the fondue parties of Hampstead. He had the endorsement of Melvyn Bragg who, under pressure to increase the ratings, had reluctantly agreed to rein in his naturally reactionary stance and, with a noticeable grimace, had presented films on credible rock acts such as the Smiths. The Smiths one could understand, but George Michael? It seemed an odd choice.

Was The South Bank Show finally opting for greater accessibility, after causing the British public to yawn through hour-long specials about Cumbrian potters and tenth-rate poets from Pontypridd? Melvyn Bragg's opening statement that George was 'the most successful pop artist of the decade' seemed to support this reasoning. Sadly, the film proved uncharacteristically gushing and Bragg, adopting a style diametrically opposed to his ever-hardening Radio Four persona, fell into a run of rather bland chitchat with the star.

The interview had taken place in and around the studio during the recording of Listen Without Prejudice and featured a smartly casual George, resplendent in Nike trainers, jogging suit and baseball cap and apparently completely at ease with the situation. And quite rightly so, as the thorny problems surrounding his career and private life were never even remotely touched on. Much of this was due to George's demand that, in an attempt to avoid tiresome tabloidesque probing into his private life, the programme should concentrate on his songwriting. To an extent, that was fine but the show, which was duly packaged and flogged as a Christmas video, proved to be little more than a somewhat cynical promotional exercise.

Accompanying the release of the album, and with an equal amount of hype, there came George's autobiography, Bare – co-written with journalist Tony Parsons – in which he announced to the world that he was withdrawing from the superstar lifestyle. A wild, bizarre, naive and somewhat unbelievable claim. How could such a thing be possible? There was no doubt that George had been, for some considerable time – in fact, probably since the day he met Mark Dean – very uncomfortable with the downside of superstardom, but it was the price one had to pay. George's dislike of being surrounded by sycophancy was understandable, but every aspect of his output – and even the actual work on the book with Parsons – could only serve to intensify that predicament.

Such was George's paradox. In truth most people in Britain sympathised with his problem – after all, they, too, were wholly fed up with tabloid stupidity – but they regarded this statement as extremely naive. Incredibly, over in Hollywood, Frank Sinatra was so moved by George's withdrawal pledge that he took the unprecedented step of putting pen to paper and astonishing everyone by sending a letter to the LA

Times. Sinatra, praised George's talent and urged him to 'dust off those gossamer wings and fly yourself to the moon. Talent must not be wasted. Those who have it must hug it, embrace it, nurture it and share it lest it be taken away from you as fast as it was loaned to you. Come on George, loosen up, swing, man.'

George's reaction to this amazing letter has not been recorded. One concludes that he must have been warmed by Sinatra's curious sentences, and warmed by the fact that one of the greatest singers of the century was openly regarding him as an equal. In reply to George's murmur of desperation had come a hugely inspiring compliment. Once again it seemed that whatever George did, it would somehow turn around and come back firmly in his favour. Although Listen Without Prejudice was generally regarded as a fine album – in recent years it has attained the level of a classic – the flurry of hit singles it spawned failed to climb the charts with the same degree of self-assurance as the Faith batch.

In November, the rocky Waiting For The Day only managed to struggle into the charts before collapsing in an exhausted heap at No 23. A month later, Freedom '90, one of George's most obvious-sounding hit records to date – used years later by Take That's Robbie Williams in a brazen attempt to kickstart his own solo career – incredibly failed to get beyond No 28 (although it did touch No 8 in the States). This was possibly the most surprising failure of George's entire career, despite the fact that the song was graced by a video featuring supermodels Naomi Campbell, Cindy Crawford and Tatiana Patitz symbolically burning his Faith-period leather jacket. Enigmatically, George stuck to his vow, and refused to appear in the video.

12 battlestations two!

This period in January 1991 also saw George flitting famously down to Brazil to perform at the Rock in Rio Two festival, taking place at the Maracana Soccer Stadium. The four-night festival contained many surprises, the most poignant being saved for the final act on the final day (28 January) when, against incredible odds, George Michael reunited with Andrew Ridgeley for a Wham! reunion set – a one-off which nevertheless set ablaze a number of 'Wham! to reunite' rumours in the British press. Ludicrous rumours, of course, for George had moved into a different universe by this time and knew that artistic regression was acceptable when performed strictly in the name of fun but must never be allowed to encroach onto his main career path.

By mid-1991 it had become clear that George's retreat from public view was not quite as severe as many people had feared. Perhaps Sinatra's message had sunk in? Or perhaps, and this is more likely, his time away from touring had rekindled his desire to perform. Never again would he embark on anything resembling the daunting size of the Faith tour. However, his 1991 outing, the Cover to Cover tour, still required considerable discipline. (Actually, it was a selection of mini-tours in selected countries – a wise alternative to trundling wearily across the entire globe.)

There were other differences, too. Recalling the refreshing nature of his appearance at the Nelson Mandela bash, George dedicated a sizeable chunk of his set to his interpretations of many of his favourite songs, from the expected Stevie Wonder and Elton John songs – creating a space for Elton to make a special 'surprise guest'

Rock in Rio

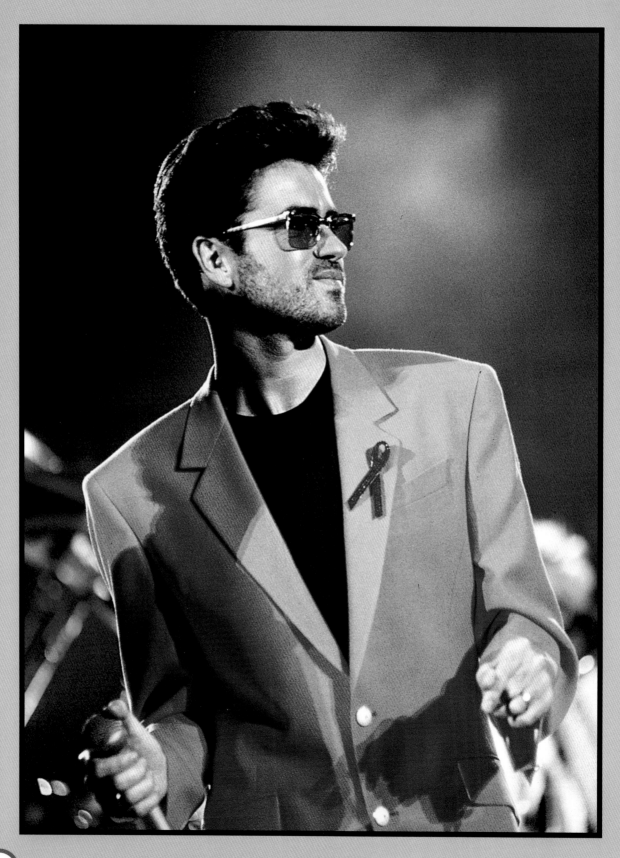

appearance – to his immensely surprising run-throughs of Adamski's Killer, Soul II Soul's Back to Life, Terence Trent D'Arby's Sign Your Name and various Seal compositions. Sensitive to the press criticisms of the Faith tour, which suggested that George's material had tended to merge together to form a 'Michael-esque' whole, he remained determined to fill the set with surprises and, most importantly, keep himself fresh.

In America, still harbouring anti-star notions, George attempted various ways of breaking down the barriers between star and audience. Invariably these attempts would prove, to his angst, futile and serve only to highlight the divide. In America, for instance, he instigated a Meet and Greet scenario, during which fans lined up two-by-two to chat to him while various record company flunkies circulated with soft drinks and matchstick pretzels. The fans, more or less plucked at random from the crowd, seemed mostly bewildered as they stammered through their allotted fifteen seconds with George and found themselves burdened with armfuls of promotional paraphernalia (sweatshirt, t-shirt, concert programme). The truth was that George's quest to break down barriers was simply hopeless. Ironically, the Cover to Cover tour would see him surrounded by more minders and assorted helpers than ever before, all attending his every whim and keeping him well and truly cocooned while his manager, Robert Kahane, flitted around, making excuses to both fans and press: 'I'm sorry, but George is just so busy.'

He was busy, or course, but never before had an artist seemed so utterly, preciously elevated. Various stars, hoping to bask in his reflected glamour, flocked to the tour, smiling before the paparazzi, pushing for coverage. In Chicago alone

– and the tour would touch thirty-five US cities – he would be visited by Michael Jordan, Dolly Parton , Aretha Franklin and, onstage, of course, Elton John. The sets would vary and, perhaps to add even more variety, a different set of backing singers would be rehearsed for each city. (In Chicago it would be the famous Edwin Hawkins Singers, darkening the gospel effects of Freedom '90.) Records were broken at New York's Madison Square Garden, where ticket receipts grossed an incredible $752,685, spread over two sell-out dates. These two concerts would later be celebrated as George's finest to date, each one stretching well over the two-and-a-half-hour limit. In them he joyously added Ain't Nobody and the triumphant Ain't No Stopping Us Now to his 'covers' sequence.

There were still worries, though. While sales of Listen Without Prejudice seemed to be going well – although not anything like as well as Faith – and his concerts seemed to sell out in every town in every country, still there were worries. The lovely Cowboys And Angels single proved too subdued for British tastes and failed to climb past No 45. Although a late release from the album and never expected to blast into the Top 10, George still regarded this as immensely disappointing and found it difficult to square it with the speed of the ticket sales for his sell-out dates at Wembley Arena.

In a sense, his worries were unfounded. His live duet with Elton John, Don't Let The Sun Go Down On Me, was about to be released as a single and surprised everyone by immediately storming to No 1 in Britain during the run-up to Christmas (the single would also top the US Charts in February 1992). This would be the year that the entire George Michael hyperbole would

The Princess of Wales meets George and kd lang while David Puttnam looks on

crumble into a bitter legal mess. Although it would be several months before his relationship with his record company, Sony, soured into absolute, irretrievable stalemate, it seems that he had already consolidated his previous 'hard' attitude, encouraged by his manager Robert Kahane. This was not necessarily a bad thing, for , George was finally beginning to use his intelligence with regard to business matters – or so he thought.

Apparently the first people to feel the sting of the new hard-line George were the hapless Chancery Financial Management. Bizarrely, George filed a £1m lawsuit against them, accusing them of poor investment advice on his

pension fund (pension fund? George Michael needs a pension fund?). His actions sent ripples of unrest through the hundreds of companies involved in the George Michael industry. Had the Bushey boy finally grown up or had he, as the industry whispers suggested, grown increasingly paranoid?

The answer, one might suggest with the benefit of hindsight, would lie somewhere in the middle. He had indeed grown up and started to take control of his own life. Curiously, his

paranoia didn't quite extend far enough, for he still relied too heavily on those close to him in particular, on his all-powerful management team. Despite this, or possibly because of it, George Michael was about to enter the strangest and perhaps the loneliest phase of his career, if not his entire life.

Since the death of the great Freddie Mercury back in November 1991, the remaining members of Queen had been busily organising a Concert for Life Aids Benefit gig, to be staged at Wembley Stadium – Freddie's favourite arena – in April 1992. Cajoling a disparate bunch of rock artists into performing wasn't difficult, for Freddie Mercury had commanded tremendous respect throughout the industry. Furthermore, following Mercury's death, much to their surprise, Queen had even become hip. Mercury's 'disposable-razor songs' (his own term) had, apparently, sunk deep into the consciousness of just about everyone who occasionally listened to pop or rock radio. Their was an intangible, childlike magic to Freddie Mercury and many people failed to realise this until after his death. George Michael, like all the others, didn't need asking twice. He had been friendly with Mercury during the previous few years and had – perhaps as a consequence – grown to love the music of Queen even more. On the day of the concert, backed by the London Community Gospel Choir, he would take great delight in performing the Queen tracks Year Of '39, Somebody To Love and, in a duet with Lisa Stansfield, These Are The Days Of Our Lives.

Lisa Stansfield: 'I think I would have to say that was the best day of my life – singing with George. I didn't know Freddie personally and, at first, felt a bit uncomfortable about that. But George told me all about him. What a fantastic person he was. It was obvious that Freddie meant so much to George, so I felt really honoured. It sounds corny but Freddie was definitely on that stage with us. You could just tell, and the crowd knew it. It was just the most incredibly moving experience. I'll never forget it and I know George won't, either.'

Three days after the performance, George Michael announced that he had donated £500,000 from the royalties of Don't Let The Sun Go Down On Me to various British and American Aids and children's educational charities. But beneath the surface, things were beginning to boil. With a view to forthcoming legal wrangles with his record company, George saw a loophole and began work on a concept album entitled Trojan Souls, a project intended to be released through his cousin Andros Georgiou's new label, Hardback Records. The idea was simple, effective and no doubt something of a wind-up for Sony. While not performing on the record himself, George would write songs to be performed by a variety of guest vocalists, including Anita Baker, Elton John, Bryan Ferry, Aretha Franklin and Stevie Wonder.

In theory, the sessions, to be recorded in Los Angeles, would stand outside the confines of the Sony contract. In effect, and perhaps obviously, the resulting press coverage caused the company to significantly harden its attitude in return. At this point, a few of George's friends began to get worried and duly warned him. He was heading towards an out-and-out legal battle. For the first time it began to dawn on the music industry, if not the press, that the situation here was evolving into something rather more serious than the standard artist versus record company sniping. It was turning nasty and George, to his own potential loss, was about to attempt the impossible and take on the mighty corporate beast of Sony.

In September 1992, it finally became clear that George Michael's two renegotiations of his contract with Sony had proved insufficient. Spurred on by his famously aggressive manager Robert Kahane, the relationship between George and Sony, which had taken over CBS before George had signed his 1988 contract, had become increasingly fraught. Finally, George, brimming with accusations, stormed into the New York offices of Sony and made it clear that, although he was tied to an eight-album deal, he would never, ever record a single note of music for them again. At that meeting he claimed that Sony had underpromoted Listen Without Prejudice and subsequently killed the album's commercial potential (Listen Without Prejudice had sold only seven million copies, approximately half the global sales of Faith). He also claimed contractual unfairness, and that Sony's earnings from his music were outstripping his own by seven to one.

Effectively this was true. George's gross worldwide earnings in the five-year period up to December 1992 had been £16.89m. Sony's share had been £95.5m. Over the same period his gross profits were £7.35m, compared to Sony's £52.45m. Breaking this down further means that, for Faith and Listen Without Prejudice, George earned just 37p per CD and 34p per cassette in Britain. Sony's profits for the same sales were £2.45 per CD and £1.49 per cassette. Not that this was unusual. The above percentages compare favourably to many lesser acts.

But at the heart of the problem was George Michael's unease with Sony's apparent 'attitude'.

After endless communications between the star and the company, significantly relayed through Kahane, Michael came to the conclusion that Sony were only capable of viewing him in commercial terms, and had no desire to encourage and enhance his natural artistic direction. Of course, this imbalanced relationship between the record company and the artist is present in every single recording contract. Indeed, such acrimony bubbles away at all times. All managers and record company A&R men are aware of it and quite often allow it to rise to the surface when it suits their particular cause. The catalyst is their star's artistic temperament – a loaded gun, dangerously poised.

One month later, George's lawyer, Tony Russell, informed Sony that George was not bound by his contract and effectively 'owned' his own music and artistic output, as well as retaining the right to decide his own artistic direction. Russell's action officially kick-started the legal war, which, Mr Justice Knox noted, would not come to court until at least October 1993. On 30 October, Russell filed a High Court action against Sony, which were disputing George's claims. This was followed by George's official 'start of war' statement.

'Since Sony corporation bought my contract, along with everything and everyone else at CBS, I have seen the great American company that I proudly signed to as a teenager become a small part of the production line for a giant electronics corporation which, quite frankly, has no understanding of the creative process. Sony appears to see artists as little more than software.'

Over in England, the tabloids scoured the country, seeking out exaggerated tales of distraught George Michael fans apparently

'George Michael thinks he's

hard done by. You should see

our fucking contract'

fellow Sony artists Manic Street Preachers

unable to face the terrifying prospect of at least three years with no new George Michael product. Interestingly enough, these vacuous reports coincided with a noticeable rise in sales of copies of both Listen Without Prejudice and Faith. People were obviously stocking up. Beneath the surface of these lightweight stories, however, lay a distinctly sad tale. A major world star was effectively paralysed by circumstance.

As such, 1993 would prove to be an artistic desert for George, very lightly peppered with notable highlights. Not for the first or the last time in his life, he would divide his time equally between Los Angeles and London, spending long, lazy afternoons walking on Hampstead Heath, accompanied only by his Labrador dog. To some extent, George found that his 'maturing' had worked. It was now possible, just, for him to wander through parts of London without being instantly mobbed by hordes of dangerously enthusiastic girls. People usually believed him to be a lookalike. After all, what would George Michael be doing on Hampstead Heath?

In April, he surfaced to take part in Aretha Franklin's TV special Duets, recorded at New York's Nederlander Theatre and networked on Fox in the US in May. By this time, and much to his surprise, George's Five Live EP, with tracks from the Freddie Mercury Tribute Concert – Somebody To Love/These Are The Days Of Our Lives (with Lisa Stansfield), plus a medley from his Cover to Cover tour of Papa Was A Rolling Stone, Killer, and his own song, Calling You – crashed dramatically into the UK charts at No 1. With the Sony dispute raging in the background, the EP was released on Hollywood Records with the proceeds, again, going to various Aids charities.

Monday 21 June 1994
The Old Bailey, London

The queue began to form at 7.30am. First three girls, huddling together in the drizzle, all squeals and fits of giggles, then six, then twelve, a swell of latent Wham! fandom, passing George Michael stories around from group to group, bravely defying the rain and hoping, more than anything else in the world, to be given a seat in the gallery of room 34. Before long, however, the girls would be outmanoeuvred by a more skillful band of onlookers, the Fleet Street photographers, who saw nothing wrong in shunting these excitable fans aside with shoulder charges, elbows, and camera bags. More accustomed to the chase, the photographers surged upon the beige Mercedes like ducks fighting for pickings of bread. They swarmed the car, backing off only as the house-sized minders lined the pathway through which an astonished and perhaps rather touched George Michael, in sunglasses, unshaven and impressively besuited, marched into the courtroom. The pop trial of the decade had, at long last, reached its climax.

George lost. Sony, and behind Sony in the shadows, the music industry, emerged triumphant. But, for a while there, it was scary. The notion of a major star turning around and accusing his record company of not understanding him, nor even attempting to treat him as an artist rather than a commercial product, was truly scary. If George had won, all hell would have been let loose. Perhaps it's a shame. George decided, naturally, to appeal against the High Court ruling that, in his words, 'would bind me in slavery until the next century'.

After the court had dismissed George's claim that Sony were in restraint of trade, he once more

Michael

vowed never to record for them again. Mr Justice Jonathan Parker produced a 273-page ruling that stressed that the Sony contract was reasonable and pointed out that George was intelligent, articulate and had had access to the best legal advice before signing. While the judge decided that the singer was refreshingly candid, he was scathing in his criticism of his manager Robert Kahane, who was considered 'thoroughly untrustworthy'. As this was read aloud, George could clearly be seen shaking his head in disbelief.

But the judge continued: 'The contract signed in 1988, after Sony had taken over CBS, was not weighed financially against George Michael. Nor was it unenforceable.'

Afterwards, George said: 'The ruling means I have no rights over my work. In fact I have no guarantee that my work will be released at all. If Sony reject my work, it will never see the light of day. There is no such thing as resignation for an

artist in the music industry. Effectively, you sign a piece of paper at the beginning of your career and you are expected to live with that decision, good or bad, for the rest of your life.'

As to the main thrust of George's case, that Sony failed to back him adequately after he had shed his sex-symbol image during the Listen Without Prejudice campaign, the judge said, 'George Michael expected a consequent change of artistic direction would, in turn, mean a loss of sales. There was no oppression or misuse of bargaining power on behalf of Sony. There was no compulsion on behalf of George Michael to sign contracts, first with CBS in 1984 and then with Sony in 1988. If his subsequent recording career proved successful, as it has done, the contracts would last for the rest of his working life and make him very rich indeed.'

At this point George, clearly distressed, could be heard sighing. He shook his head and glumly averted his gaze, looking downwards, aware that he was facing legal defeat.

The judge continued: 'It would be unjust to Sony if the 1988 agreement was now treated as void. Michael's best interests were not served by Mr Kahane, whose advice to the singer had been coloured by his own financial difficulties. Mr Kahane negotiated an advance of £1m so he could earn his commission. It was also in Mr Kahane's interests that Mr Michael should break with Sony and enter into fresh negotiation. Mr Kahane adopted a hostile attitude towards Sony, continually complaining to the company while, at the same time, sowing in Michael's mind the notion that Sony was acting in bad faith and spitefully towards him, feeding him with exaggerated and misleading reports about Sony's activities. I cannot help feeling that if Sony had seen more of Mr Michael and rather less of Mr Kahane, events might have turned out differently.'

It had taken just twenty minutes. George, surrounded by minders, carers, photographers, fans, police and press, looked like a boxer walking in defeat back to the dressing room. He swayed from the room. For once, the photographers on the outside were neatly duped. The beige Mercedes swept one way while George Michael hurriedly rushed to a different exit, hurling himself into a waiting grey Jaguar. Not fast enough, however, to prevent the car being instantly swamped by a mass of fans and late photographers. A comical interlude saw four giant bodyguards surrounding the vehicle, forging a parting of the waves, ushering the car away, Sweeney-style, with the words: 'Move move move!'

Behind the car, stunned, and quivering with nerves, stood George's parents Lesley and Jack,

fending off a flood of press questions and seemingly unable to take in the speed and surreal nature of the morning's events. Strange, too, was the sight of Robert Kahane emerging grim-faced from the courts, pugnaciously shunting through the crowds.

The carnival, however, was far from over. Once freed from the elastic pull of crowd, the Jaguar sped swiftly across to the nearby Howard hotel, where a press conference had been arranged. Alas, the hotel staff, apparently expecting a small, mild-mannered gathering of 'the gentlemen of the press', had arranged nothing more than a few chairs in a tiny room.

Anarchy prevailed as more than a hundred photographers and 150 journalists surged feverishly into the hotel foyer, breaking down hastily arranged signs and cramming noisily into the adjacent corridor. The photographers, naturally determined to capture George mid-speech, forced their way into the room, scattering hotel staff this way and that. George, stunned and angered, brusquely ordered them to leave. 'I'm shocked and extremely disappointed,' the singer shouted. Nobody, of course, knew whether he was talking about the High Court ruling or the appalling behaviour of the press.

The music industry, of course, expressed a collective sigh of relief. Had George won, the floodgates would have been opened and the aforementioned delicate relationship between company and artist would have raged in a hundred different courtrooms. For the music industry this would have been a legal world war and one which, for anyone that was not a lawyer, would have been truly expensive. Could anyone truly be the victor in such a legal quagmire? Opinion was divided. And representatives from

George with 'companion' Kay Beckenham

both sides of this divide would waste no time in putting their views forward.

In The Times Jonathan King, forever defending the ruthless heart of the music business, stated: 'George Michael is being just naive and churlish. If he hadn't signed that contract he would still have been a Greek waiter.' A stupid and inaccurate statement, but one that seemed to capture the sympathy of the British press. The music industry mogul Pete Waterman added: 'Anyone who has £70m and claims to be hard done by should look at the rail strike.' The September 1994 issue of Q magazine sensibly kept its opinions away from the debate and published a page full of entertaining and varying opinion from a wide selection of artists. Here is a brief taste.

The Manic Street Preachers (George's fellow Sony artists): 'George Michael thinks he's hard done by. You should see our fucking contract.'

Prince: 'Artistic freedom is all that matters. An artist has to be true to his art. Why can't George Michael do whatever he wants? Why can't he write a ballet if he wants to? Why should he be shackled, a slave to marketing?'

Tori Amos: 'There are always going to be two opposing sides – the artist's side and the record company's side. The two will never meet. They think we are brats. We think they're expensive, stinky-cheese schmoozers.'

Damon Albarn of Blur: 'Many of the people I knew in the legal profession knew he wasn't going to win before he even started.'

Marcella Detroit: 'George Michael has a genuine grievance. No record company should be able to own the artist's copyright. Considering the cost and the many other heinous clauses that exist within these contracts, George's advisers should have been aware of the likely outcome and advised him accordingly. As things stand, there is no victory. Not for Sony, not for George and, most importantly, not for the fans.'

25 June 1995

For once, it seemed that the music business whispers had been correct. Most people inside or on the periphery of the business were saying that Sony had accepted the fact that the differences between themselves and George Michael would never be healed and that it would be pointless to lock him into a contractual artistic prison. Despite their public claim that 'we have great respect for George Michael and hope to be working within him again in the future', they had been talking for some time with the large companies that were hovering with contractual intent.

The decision to finally 'release' him was eventually triggered by George's insistence that he would spend a sizeable chunk of his £70m fortune taking the case to the European court. Fearing an elongated and needlessly expensive showdown, Sony decided to encourage offers. This fact became obvious in June 1995 when, after a year of solid negotiations, George Michael agreed to a deal that would at long last mercifully bring to a close this acrimonious dispute. He was to sign a new multimillion-pound contract with Virgin, Dreamworks and SK6, the new entertainment group set up by Steven Spielberg, ex-Disney boss Jeffrey Katzenberg and music mogul David Geffen. This astronomical, ground-breaking deal would be the first and flagship signing for the embryonic conglomerate, founded with the collective fortunes of three of the industry's most charismatic figures. As the news broke, it was revealed that George had already started working on his new album at a secret location in Los Angeles. This in itself was a brave move as although agreed in principle, the new contract was still at a delicate stage of negotiations.

Understandably perhaps, George's new record company approached the matter with 'open-minded firmness'. It was, after all, a huge investment. They would pay Sony £10m, literally to 'buy' the star. On top of this, Sony would continue to cream 2 to 3 per cent from all George's future royalties.

George and Sharon Stone

Michael

13 — Older

Pop music may have altered irrevocably since the release of Listen Without Prejudice, Volume One but, with the advent of the long-awaited album Older, it seemed that George Michael's music had remained suspended in a state of blueish elegance, of majestic dips and surges. This is no put-down. For Older was, in so many respects, Listen Without Prejudice Volume Two, a masterpiece of introversion and, once again, the absolute antithesis of everything Wham! had stood for.

Michael-ologists – a growing army these days after scrutinising his legal battles – would have to wait until the final funky track had almost staggered to an impromptu halt to hear the eagerly anticipated words, 'Feels good to be free'. And, even then, they came in a whisper. It was as if George had tried, had really tried to keep such strong feelings suppressed but unable, alas, to control himself any more, had blurted them out just before the funky conclusion.

The album's title promised a great deal. Older – six years older. And wiser? Possibly. But how could it be possible to make a pop record displaying more maturity than Listen Without Prejudice? That, frankly, was George's only real quandary. The music would have to continue as if the entire Sony mess, and the last six years, had never happened. Not unexpectedly, a mighty comeback single, Jesus To A Child, opened the proceedings, solemnly guiding you into the album and, like Praying For Time, it was hastily followed by a more sprightly single, on this occasion Fastlove, the most untypical song on the album.

Fastlove, in spirit and style, is chart-friendly

funk, an elder relation of Everything She Wants. It sounds – and nothing else on the album evokes this sentiment – like mature Wham!. As such it does tend to wrongfoot the first-time listener who is, literally, brought back into the swing of things with the delicate, reflective title track, complete with a Miles Davis-like blue trumpet.

The more upbeat Spinning The Wheel connects with two other tracks, To Be Forgiven and The Strangest Thing, to exude a feel of conservative arrogance. This is George Michael in cruise mode, a serene artist in complete and absolute control of his craft. And if none of these three tracks actually evokes a spirit of adventure, this is balanced by the comforting feel that, at least in the little world of George Michael albums, everything is in order, everything is progressing exactly as planned.

One sees young to middle-aged couples, made blurry by wine, settling down in a post-meal haze under soft lights with Older politely flowing out of the speakers. The aforementioned link with Miles Davis might well have been highly significant, for Davis' better, later work excelled in such soft tones. Who, other than brash, young, naive and rather stupid rock critics, could suggest that music of credible artistry could not be constructed within this much-maligned area?

But critics – the better critics in England, from the more mature end of the music press – did tend to feel that Older, for all its intriguing twists and faint shadows, wasn't quite as interesting as Listen Without Prejudice. Frankly, it couldn't possibly break any further into self-conscious soul searching without pushing into areas of unforgivable pretentiousness. In fact, as it is, George Michael does stand charged, at times, of taking himself little too seriously, of confusing personal intensity with solemnity, and once past the punchy Fastlove there isn't a great deal of lightheartedness on the album. How strange, then, to discover a song deep into the record – Star People – that turns out to be a blatant attack on celebrities who attempt to impose their problems on their respective audiences. What a curious song to come from a talent so delicately poised on the verge of pretentiousness.

Those first-time listeners, once past the mighty opening foursome of Jesus To A Child, Fastlove, Older and Spinning The Wheel, might have allowed their attention to wander as the album moved softly onwards – and to be honest, there is a slight dip – but this would be a great shame, for they could so easily have missed the album's true, unexpected gem, a song called You Have Been Loved, which lurks near the album's funky conclusion. The sentiment, ushered in by that blue trumpet again, is the most melancholy and, as Q magazine's Paul Du Noyer noted, possibly the loveliest thing he has ever written. It is also undoubtedly the deepest. Here we find a character – presumably George – bonding with the mother of his bereaved friend. And not for one second is the listener tempted to doubt the singer's sincerity. George, unlike, say, Morrissey, is a stranger to flippancy and couldn't possibly play with such a dangerous lyrical device.

As a whole, Older is an extremely enticing record, which improves in its beauty with repeated plays. I will be unpopular for suggesting this, but I feel it is his finest, most complete record to date. And indeed, few people could argue with the notion that in Faith, Listen Without Prejudice and Older, George Michael has maintained an extraordinary level of quality, especially among those at the very peak of the commercial pop world. Oddly, though, and quite unlike his peers, his music tends to work better in album form, when the songs are stacked closely together, often merging dreamily.

As far as British radio is concerned, George Michael, again rather ironically, now seems to be something of an outsider. Whereas, say, Simply Red have linked themselves cleverly with the chart-friendly familiarity of soft rappers the Fugees, George has remained aloof. This thought hits me as I type. In the background, Simon Mayo, Radio One's mild-mannered mid-morning man, has just followed Bush's admittedly rather wonderful Swallowed with George's Fastlove. The jolt is just too much, especially as the Spice Girls weigh in to complete an extraordinary threesome. But it is George Michael who – to his immense credit, I believe – is the odd one out. Again, quite the antithesis of the radio-friendly Wham!.

Michael

Michael

George

February 1997,

and the raging orgy of showbiz horror known to Britain, if not elsewhere, as the Brits, stormed into the media on a wave of hype every bit as ferocious as the preceding year's event, during which Jarvis Cocker had famously lurched onto the stage during Michael Jackson's hugely condescending performance. Cocker's actions had alerted the media to the notion that the Brits was an event simply crammed full of potential stories. The 1997 Brits belonged, as far as the press were concerned, to the Spice Girls, who upstaged even their own excellent performance with a bit of press-grabbing nipple-flashing, while receiving the award for Best Single.

Elsewhere, most people were delighted to see the tragedy-stricken Manic Street Preachers defying all the odds to clinch the Best Group and Best Album awards. The Brits, if nothing else, is a reasonable barometer for testing the trends of the moment – and only of the moment. How significant, then, that Best Male Artist, in the wake of Older, was given to George Michael, eleven years or so after Wham! had relinquished their dominance of British pop music.

George's apparent delight, however, was well and truly clouded by deep family sorrow. For his cancer-stricken mother, Lesley, was edging towards premature death in a London hospital. Things had seemed to improve during the preceding Christmas period and, to the delight of Melanie, Yioda and Jack, she had been allowed home for the festivities. But the relief was brief. For George, his proud Brits achievement had been well and truly placed in perspective. Needless to say, he couldn't possibly attend, and left his great friend Elton John to collect the award on his behalf. George's message was simple and

Michael

George

with Naomi Campbell

respectful: 'I would have loved to have been there,' he said, 'and say thank you to everybody who has made music part of my life for fifteen years.'

Music, fittingly, would drift into George's statement regarding the untimely death of his mother, delivered as he attended a Capital Radio awards ceremony in March in aid of the charity, Help a London Child. 'My mother was a woman of great compassion,' he stated. 'She felt we were living in a world that was being drained of that. She was incredibly proud that music could inspire people to give money to this cause. As long as I was able to communicate with my mother our point of reference was the radio. I remember being 12 years old and obsessed with Queen. When Bohemian Rhapsody came on the radio when it was No 1, it was always time for dinner. My mother told me many times that if she wanted to hear my voice and I wasn't around, she had only to turn on the radio and there I was.'

Michael

Michael

George and his dad and mum, Jack and Lesley Panayiotou

'My mother was a woman of great compassion. She felt we were living in a world that was being drained of that'

Endpiece

From the Express, Monday 31 March 1997
By Jason Solomons

George Michael made a £166,000 donation to a children's charity yesterday. The singer telephoned DJ Chris Tarrant's show on London's Capital Radio to pledge his money, which took the total raised beyond £1m.

His generosity made the station's Help a London Child weekend its most successful since the charity was launched in 1980.

George had already written and recorded a song specially for the event. Waltz Away Dreaming was made in memory of his mother, Lesley, who died from cancer last month. Listeners pledged £35,000 to hear the unreleased song. George, 33, had already chipped in £70,000, but when he heard the total had reached £904,000, he donated another £96,000. He said: 'I hope everyone who listens to the song appreciates what it means to me. I didn't think I'd have a good day like this for a long time. I had a fantastic time just listening to the radio.'

George has recently been seen helping at London soup kitchens.

Discography

Singles

Wham! Rap (Enjoy What You Do)
Innervision IVLA 2442/June 1982
(Reissued January 1983)
UK Chart Position 8

Young Guns (Go For It)
Innervision IVLA 2766/September 1982
UK Chart Position 3

Bad Boys
Innervision IVLA 3134/May 1983
UK Chart Position 2

Club Tropicana
Innervision IVLA 3613/July 1983
UK Chart Position 4

Club Fantastic Megamix
Innervision IVLA 3586/November 1983
UK Chart Position 15

Wake Me Up Before You Go Go
Epic A 4440/May 1984
UK Chart Position 1

Freedom
Epic A 4743/October 1984
UK Chart Position 1

Last Christmas
Epic GA 4949/December 1984
UK Chart Position 2

I'm Your Man
Epic A 6716/November 1985
UK Chart Position 1

The Edge Of Heaven
Epic Fin 1/June 1986
UK Chart Position 1

Last Christmas (Pudding mix)/Where Did Your Heart Go?
Epic 650 269/December 1986

Albums

Fantastic
Innervision IVL 25328/July 1983
UK Chart Position 1
Bad Boys / A Ray Of Sunshine / Love Machine / Club Tropicana / Wham! Rap (Enjoy What You Do) / Nothing Looks The Same In The Light / Young Guns (Go For It).

Make It Big
Epic EPC 86311/November 1984
UK Chart Position 1
Wake Me Up Before You Go Go / Everything She Wants / Like A Baby / Freedom / If You Were There / Credit Card Baby / Careless Whisper.

The Final
Epic/October 1986
UK Chart Position 1
Wham! 2. Also released on gold disc in a collectors' box, with T-shirt, notebook, pencil, calendar and numbered certificate. Wham! Rap (Enjoy What You Do) / Young Guns (Go For It) / Bad Boys / Club Tropicana / Wake Me Up Before You Go Go / Where Did Your Heart Go? / Careless Whisper / Freedom / Everything She Wants / Last Christmas / I'm Your Man / Battlestations / Blue (Armed With Love) / A Different Corner / The Edge Of Heaven.

Singles

Careless Whisper
Epic A 4603/ July 1984
UK Chart Position 1

A Different Corner
Epic A 7033/March 1986
UK Chart Position 1

I Knew You Were Waiting (For Me)
With Aretha Franklin Epic Duet 2
January 1987
UK Chart Position 1

I Want Your Sex
Epic Lust 1/June 1987
UK Chart Position 3

Faith
Epic EMU 3/October 1987
UK Chart Position 2

Father Figure
Epic EMU 4/December 1987
UK Chart Position 2

One More Try
Epic EMU 5/April 1988
UK Chart Position 8

Monkey
Epic EMU 6/July 1988
UK Chart Position 13

Kissing A Fool
 Epic EMU 7/November 1988
UK Chart Position 18

Praying For Time
Epic GEO 1/August 1990
UK Chart Position 6

Waiting For The Day
Epic GEO 2 /October 1990
UK Chart Position 23

Freedom '90
Epic GEO/3 December 1990
UK Chart Position 28

Heal The Pain
Epic GEO 4/February 1991
UK Chart Position 31

Cowboys And Angels
Epic GEO 5/March 1991
UK Chart Position 45

Don't Let The Sun Go Down On Me
(With Elton John)November 1991
UK Chart Position 1

solo

Too Funky
Epic GEO 6/June 1992
UK Chart Position 4

Five Live EP
(With Queen and Lisa Stansfield)
HG 61479/April 1993
Somebody To Love / These Are The Days Of Our
Lives / Calling You / Papa Was A Rolling Stone /
Killer (Medley)
UK Chart Position 1

Jesus To A Child
VSCDG 1571/January 1996
UK Chart Position 1

Fastlove
VSCDG 1570/April 1996
UK Chart Position 1

Spinning The Wheel
EP VSCDG 1579/September 1996
UK Chart Position 2
Spinning The Wheel / You Know That I Want To
/ Safe / Spinning The Wheel (Forthright Mix)

Older
EP VSCDG 1626/January 1997
UK Chart Position 10

Star People '97
VSCDG 1674/April 1997

Albums

Faith
Epic 631 5224/November 1987
UK Chart Position 1
Faith / Father Figure / I Want Your Sex (Parts 1
and 2) / Monkey / One More Try / Hand To
Mouth / Look At Your Hands / Kissing A Fool

Listen Without Prejudice, Volume One
Epic 467 2952/August 1990
UK Chart Position 1
Praying For Time / Freedom '90 / They Won't
Go When I Go / Something To Save / Cowboys
And Angels / Waiting For The Day / Mother's
Pride / Heal The Pain / Soul Free / Waiting (Reprise)

Older
Virgin LC 3098/April 1996
UK Chart Position 1
Jesus To A Child / Fastlove / Older / Spinning
The Wheel / It Doesn't Matter Anymore /
Strangest Thing / To Be Forgiven / Move On /
Star People / You Have Been Loved / Free

With Elton John

Wrap Her Up/Restless
Rocket EJS 10/November 1985

{ George Michael can also be heard on Elton John's single, 'Nikita', David Cassidy's 'Last Kiss' , Boogie Box High's 'Jive Talkin' and Deon Estus's solo album, 'Spell'. }

chapter one
Johnny Rogan **Wham! The Death Of A Supergroup** (Omnibus Press)
Bruce Dessau **George Michael: The Making Of A Superstar** (Pan)
Dave McCullouch **Sounds**

chapter two
Dave McCullouch **Sounds**
Ian Penman **NME**

chapter three
Simon Garfield **Time Out**
Simon Garfield **Expensive Habits** (Faber And Faber)

chapter four
Paul Morley **NME**
Johnny Rogan **Wham! The Death Of A Supergroup** (Omnibus Press)
Tony Parsons **Bare**
Dave McCullouch **Sounds**

chapter five
Tony Parsons **The Face**

chapter six
Ian Cranna **Smash Hits**
Paul Morley **NME**
Ian Birch **Melody Maker**
Simon Garfield **Time Out**

chapter seven
John Blake **The Sun**
Rick Sky **Daily Star**
Gill Pringle **The Mirror**

chapter eight
Rolling Stone Magazine
Rick Sky **Daily Star**
John Blake **The Sun**
Danny Kelly **NME**

chapter nine
The Times
The Sun
Tony Parsons **The Face**

chapter ten
Time Out
Gill Pringle **The Mirror**
Dave Hill **The Guardian**

chapter eleven
Tony Parsons **The Face**
The Sun

chapter twelve
Karen Krizanovich **Sky Magazine**
Ian Dooley **Replay**
Richard Duce **The Times**
Mathew Lyon and Rufus Obius **The Sunday Times**
Joe Joseph **The Times**
David Toop **Arena**
Q Magazine

chapter thirteen
Paul Du Noyer **Q Magazine**

chapter fourteen
Claudia Joseph **The Express**
Jason Solomons **The Express**
The Sun

picture credits

Pictorial Press – pages 5, 7, 39
London Features International – pages 13, 22, 89
Retna – pages 21, 26
Scope Features – pages 26, 33, 35, 53, 75
Fryderyk Gabowicz/Redferns – page 27
David Parker/Alpha – page 29
Rex Features – pages 30, 77, 82, 109
Alan Davidson/Alpha – page 37
Walter McBribe/Retna – page 43
Chris Craymer/Scope Features – page 49
Michael Putland/Retna – pages 50, 59, 78 (top), 81
Erik Heinila/Shooting Star/Scope Features – page 55
Dave Hogan/Rex Features – page 60
Neal Preston/Retna – page 65
Eugene Adebari/London Features International – page 67
Eddie Malluk/Retna – page 68
Kevin Mazur/London Features International – pages 70, 85, 86, 87, 99, 107
Adrian Boot/Retna – page 78 (bottom)
Davies & Starr/Retna – page 91
Alpha – pages 95 (top), 98, 104
Andre Camara/Alpha – page 102
Richard Chambury/Alpha – page 106
Mick Hutson/Redferns – pages 95 (bottom), 110, 118 (top), 120, 123
Kieran Doherty/Redferns – pages 113, 119
Larry Busacca/Retna – page 114
Dave Benett/Alpha – pages 115, 118 (bottom)
Peter Lessing/London Features International – page 117
Ron Wolfson/London Features International – page 121
Steve Finn/Alpha – page 122
David Fisher/London Features International – page 125
Chris Taylor/Retna – page 126

Picture Research by Odile Schmitz